real-world messiness. Each section offers us new ideas for creative encounters that spark curiosity and courage for educators and students alike. Goodwin models the iron rule he presents: guiding–not prescribing. He shows educators how to empower themselves and to scaffold the kinds of learning experiences that help students to think and act for themselves.

—**Annie Rappeport**, *PhD, Associate Director of Community Dialogue, Yale University*

Teach Like a Community Organizer is a refreshing guide for educators who want to inspire agency and collaboration in their classrooms. It blends practical strategies with deep respect for students, reminding teachers that idealism and real-world teaching can go hand in hand.
—**Carol Burris**, *Executive Director of The Network for Public Education*

Teach Like a Community Organizer is a heart-filled, determined look at teaching students to be active in learning. Jacob Goodwin grounds his unit design in place and investigation, and most importantly, in the students in the room. I inhaled this book like the deep breath you take at the peak of a mountain. Walking beside a teacher who thinks about our work in complex ways and is constantly learning, agitated by his curiosity, empowered me. Dare we teach like this? Let your answer be YES.
—**Penny Kittle**, *author of* Book Love, Micro Mentor Texts, *and* 180 Days

With vibrant anecdotes, thoughtful analysis, and practical exercises, *Teach Like a Community Organizer* is a book to inspire and guide educators looking to center humanity and connection by building profound community within and beyond the classroom.
—**Michaela Brant**, *The Progressive magazine*

In a time where education has focused increasingly on the individual, Jacob Goodwin's *Teach Like a Community Organizer* offers an urgent corrective. This book reminds us that education is inherently social and is built on trusting relationships cemented through meaningful action. Goodwin keeps us firmly planted in the "world as it is," as we witness his students assessing their local waterways, problem-solving plastic waste, mapping their communities, and conducting mock trials. With its clear anecdotes and concrete activities, this book offers civic-minded educators a framework for engaging in place-based learning that forges the community of young citizens our world is crying for.
—**Pablo Wolfe**, *co-author of* The Civically Engaged Classroom: Reading, Writing, and Speaking for Change

Teach Like a Community Organizer should be required reading for educators. Filled with tips and tools for cultivating an organizer's mindset, this essential volume is aimed at helping teachers reclaim their agency by reinvigorating the idealism that made them want to teach in the first place. I hear regularly from educators who want to know how they can hold onto hope in a hostile world. Now I have an answer. Read this book!
—**Jennifer C. Berkshire**, *author of* A Wolf at the Schoolhouse Door *and* The Education Wars: A Citizen's Guide and Defense Manual

Jake Goodwin writes that our conversations create the world. That wisdom, and this fine book, can help create that better world.
— **Richard Louv**, *author of* Last Child in the Woods *and* Our Wild Calling

Teaching and community organizing may sound like quite different professions, but both aim at equipping people to work together for a better world. As a practitioner of both trades, I've long wanted a book that would make the case that Jake Goodwin makes here. Drawing on stories from his own experience, he bridges the gap between theory and practice with a pedagogy I find inspiring. If you're concerned about the future of American education and our civic life, you'll find a toolkit for reform and rebuilding between these covers.
—**Parker J. Palmer**, *author of* Healing the Heart of Democracy, Let Your Life Speak, *and* The Courage to Teach

Jacob Goodwin's new book, *Teach Like a Community Organizer*, is exactly what the doctor ordered for those finding themselves trying to teach in uncertain times. Goodwin effectively weaves together stories, practical know-how and ready to use activities that can be used as written or customized with ease. The result is a treasury of ideas that are all at once meaningful, memorable, and genuinely fun. What sets Goodwin's work apart is how he takes readers outside, into the mud, to see the beauty and glean the wisdom that can only come from engagement in

Teach Like a Community Organizer

This book is an invitation to participate in the "world as it is" with your students. When you teach like a community organizer, you help your students to notice the world as it is, to dream about the world as it should be, and to move toward closing the gap between the two. With this book, you will be able to:

- Develop the mindset of a community organizer
- Apply organizing concepts to the classroom
- Determine how you can make a difference in supporting progressive change in your own school and community
- Take action in bringing democratic practices to your own school

For teachers who have been witness to attacks on public education in the past few years and feel like something needs to change, but are unsure of what to do or are dismayed by the enormity of the size of the problems that we are facing, this book provides tools and examples for direct application to the classroom. The book encourages teachers to try organizing methods in their teaching, building community in the classroom and beyond.

This is an excellent resource for any teacher who has the desire to create a more holistic vision for teaching, learning and civic life, particularly for Social Studies educators and those teaching civic engagement.

Jacob Goodwin is a Social Studies educator with over a decade of experience in public schools. A 2015 James Madison Memorial Fellow, Mr. Goodwin was recognized in 2021 as the NH History Teacher of the Year. In 2023, he was named a Progressive Education Fellow for his advocacy work for public schools and was one of the 23 teachers nationally selected for the Peace Teacher Program at the United States Institute of Peace, a nonpartisan, independent institute founded by Congress with a mission to help prevent, mitigate and resolve violent conflicts. Mr. Goodwin has also been honored as an Innovator in Civic Education Fellow by the David Mathews Center for Civic Life.

Also Available from Routledge Eye On Education
(www.routledge.com/eyeoneducation)

Teaching LGBTQ+ History in High Schools: Practical Strategies and Voices of Experience
Stacie Brensilver Berman & Robert Cohen

Teaching Media Literacy with Social Media News: Practical Techniques for Middle and High School Classrooms
Roy S. Whitehurst

Teaching Women's History: Breaking Barriers and Undoing Male Centrism in K-12 Social Studies
Kelsie Brook Eckert

Teaching for CHANGE in the ELA Classroom: Integrating Social Justice and Critical Literacy for Grades 9-12
Dan Stockwell

Integrating Inquiry in Social Studies Classrooms
Carolyn Weber and Heather Hagan

The Antiracist English Language Arts Classroom
Keisha Rembert

Pop Culture Literacies: Teaching Interpretation, Response, and Composition in a Digital World
Mia Hood

Teach Like a Community Organizer

Practical Tools for Community-Building, Civic Engagement, and Progressive Change

Jacob Goodwin

NEW YORK AND LONDON

Designed cover image: Youme Nguyen Ly

First published 2026
by Routledge
605 Third Avenue, New York, NY 10158

and by Routledge
4 Park Square, Milton Park, Abingdon, Oxon, OX14 4RN

Routledge is an imprint of the Taylor & Francis Group, an informa business

© 2026 Jacob Goodwin

The right of Jacob Goodwin to be identified as author of this work has been asserted in accordance with sections 77 and 78 of the Copyright, Designs and Patents Act 1988.

All rights reserved. No part of this book may be reprinted or reproduced or utilised in any form or by any electronic, mechanical, or other means, now known or hereafter invented, including photocopying and recording, or in any information storage or retrieval system, without permission in writing from the publishers.

For Product Safety Concerns and Information please contact our EU representative GPSR@taylorandfrancis.com. Taylor & Francis Verlag GmbH, Kaufingerstraße 24, 80331 München, Germany.

Trademark notice: Product or corporate names may be trademarks or registered trademarks, and are used only for identification and explanation without intent to infringe.

ISBN: 978-1-041-19691-4 (hbk)
ISBN: 978-1-041-19688-4 (pbk)
ISBN: 978-1-003-71287-9 (ebk)

DOI: 10.4324/9781003712879

Typeset in Palatino
by KnowledgeWorks Global Ltd.

For my wife

Contents

Meet the Author xii

Introduction 1

1 One-on-One Meetings 5

2 People before Program: How Starting with Place
   Helps Make Change Pocket Sized 48

3 Agitate, Agitate, Agitate 100

4 The Iron Rule: Forging a Path Together 145

5 Make Connections Locally 193

Meet the Author

Jacob Goodwin is a Social Studies educator with over a decade of experience in public schools. A 2015 James Madison Memorial Fellow, Mr. Goodwin was recognized in 2021 as the NH History Teacher of the Year. In 2023, he was named a Progressive Education Fellow for his advocacy work for public schools and was one of the 23 teachers nationally selected for the Peace Teacher Program at the United States Institute of Peace, a nonpartisan, independent institute founded by Congress with a mission to help prevent, mitigate and resolve violent conflicts. Mr. Goodwin has also been honored as an Innovator in Civic Education Fellow by the David Mathews Center for Civic Life.

He can be reached on LinkedIn: https://www.linkedin.com/in/commongoodwin/.

Introduction

My first year of teaching, I was handed a thick binder filled with curriculum on American history. The blue covered three-ring binder was both distressing and distressed. How would I ever be able to read through this jam-packed, minutely planned curriculum while also covering the accompanying 400-page textbook? It seemed impossible. It was impossible. So, like many who had walked similar halls, and dreamed the idealistic dreams of early teacherhood, I departed from the textbook.

Today, it can be easy to lose your idealism. The world and our politics are in shambles. Yet, there can be nothing more important than keeping your idealistic vision as a teacher. Without the vision of the world and the classroom as it "should be", we slip into cynicism and the pressures to conform to the policy and curriculum pressures of the day. And if there is one thing that we teachers know, it's that policy and curriculum changes—Will. Never. Stop.

Keeping hold of your idealism does not mean living in the "world as it should be". That would be a disaster. It would be a life of unrealistic expectations for our students, selves and colleagues. It would be constant frustration over things that we can't yet change.

Teaching like an organizer is all about the application of the principle that we need to have the vision for the world as it should be—while operating and meeting people in the world as it is. The gap between these ideas—the world as it should be and the world as it is—and the desire to close that gap—is the driving force for action today. We become upset about the litter around our school and decide that we will be the ones to pick it up. Acknowledging that this doesn't solve the root cause of the problem, and that it doesn't solve the issue of litter once and for all, but by taking action, we are learning how we act together, and when we are acting together, we are learning together, and we are learning how we rebuild community together.

DOI: 10.4324/9781003712879-1

Like an object that is once in motion stays in motion, the citizen who takes action stays in action—and the community that learns to problem-solve together builds the kind of momentum that it takes to make a difference. We slowly learn from our success. We quickly learn from our mistakes as we gain a sense of agency, a sense that we can make a difference in our lives and the lives of those in our community.

Teaching like a community organizer is non-ideological. In fact, ideology and community organizing really don't mix. One of the tenets of community organizing, which will be referred to throughout this book, is to meet people where they are in the world as it is. It is from meeting people where they are that the community organizer works to find out what kind of future the community wants for itself. There is no predetermined outcome, there is only the democratic process of determining what to work together on to achieve. Trust in people and a deep commitment to listening serve as the core of teaching like a community organizer.

I found teaching like an organizer in part due to my disposition as a teacher who listens. It's a trait that I think many in our profession share. We listen to our students each day. Over the course of my 15 years in public schools, I tried to get outside of my own classroom to see if what I was hearing was what others were hearing as well. My curiosity brought me to work in service learning programs in places like Chicago, Washington, DC, and the Bay Area. It also brought me to get engaged with my union. What I experienced outside of the classroom was that teachers and communities all over were doing their best with what they had. Not only that, but there was a prideful sense of purpose exhibited by those taking action to improve their classrooms and their neighborhoods. It was something that I recognized from my own upbringing in rural New England where the "Spirit of Yankee ingenuity" was celebrated.

There was something incredibly empowering to see the unifying capacity of everyday people approaching improving their immediate surroundings with a common mindset. Still, I wasn't sure what to make of it or how to do much more than try to replicate parts and pieces of what I observed in my own classroom.

I later learned that this kind of contemplative experimentation is what the famed community organizer Ed Chambers (2008), whose words are echoed throughout this text, called "mulling about". *Teaching like a Community* is my attempt at pulling together lessons from my teaching experience using organizing frameworks and tools. You'll find examples from work with elementary through high school students—and it's my hope that these pages will provide a useful approach to teaching a diverse set of subjects.

The book is divided into five core principles from community organizing. Chapter 1 focuses on the one-on-one meeting as a foundational concept, how to "tune in" to your senses and methods for structuring productive conversations in the classroom. Chapter 2 looks at the critical role relationship building plays in creating a learning community and ways to help foster a positive sense of place. Chapter 3 examines agitation in the educational context. Chapter 4 applies the "Iron rule" of organizing, don't do for others what they can do for themselves, to the classroom in the pursuit of creating more self-direction and learner engagement. Chapter 5 considers ways to grow our practice with and into the community, different types of community partnerships and how to get started with a partnership.

Teaching like a community organizer, above all, is needed now. Organizing is the work of everyday people coming together to address the issues that matter most to their lives. It is a way of reclaiming our agency starting in the common places that we all share. Given the heightened attacks on public schools and teaching as a profession, there may be no more important commonplace for the work of the teacher-as-organizer than what was once referred to as the "common school".

Teaching like an organizer includes using methods that will be discussed in this book. These methods are meant to be applied flexibly to fit the needs of the people and places where we live. Our work in the months and years ahead will be challenging, there can be no doubt. And for that reason, it is important to be clear that methods alone are not enough. In addition, we must practice a public facing faith in people, in students and in their ability to be resilient, to grow and to reclaim common ground—in the face of hardship, intolerance and change.

This book is an invitation to participate. It's an invitation to teach like an organizer, to help your students to notice the world as it is, to dream about the world as it should be and to move toward closing the gap between the two. Every inch we claim in closing the gap between the world as it is and the world as it should be is a step toward restoring common ground today. This is a call to reclaim common ground in each and every community across our country and world. It starts with noticing our heart, head and gut.

Work Cited

Chambers, E. T. (2008). *The body trumps the brain*. ACTA Publishers.

1

One-on-One Meetings

The Teacher and Classroom as Public Life

We are part of public life as teachers. Now, the question is what can we do about it? And how can we become more effective in what we are doing?

The books were taken from my classroom. They were a collection of titles meant to help students learn about the vast diversity that is the human experience. I had never anticipated a law being passed in New Hampshire, the *"live free or die state"*, that would lead to books being plucked off our shelves. Yet, it can happen here. It has happened here.

We think of our work as teachers as public service. It is. But in recent years, the polarization and the coarsening of public life have made public service more difficult than ever. Even in bucolic New Hampshire, my home state, known for its live and let live attitude, the train has gone off the tracks. The State Department of Education set up a portal for the public to report on teachers who dared to teach about racism, for goodness sake! We, as teachers, had little guidance as to what was prohibited in terms of content and no idea what could get us reported. With the threat of having our teaching credentials stripped away and losing our livelihoods, it was apparent that—the political poison of polarization had seeped in through the school house door.

There can be no doubt that we are part of public life as teachers, especially right now. We find ourselves in a point of cultural inflection—a whirlwind moment of change where the next several decades of school life and civic life are being written. The question is: what are we doing about it? And how can we become more effective in what we are doing?

The one-on-one conversation as an essential building block for the community organizer will be discussed in this chapter.

How Do We Move between the Worlds?

Developing our heart, head and gut is a step toward navigating the space between the world as it is and the world as it should be. School has traditionally focused on developing the head. Students are asked to think analytically, write without the use of personal pronouns and to be work-force oriented. Think about it, what is one of the most frequently asked questions of young people: what do you want to be when you grow up?

Such a question seems so practical to us adults. After all, we spend so much of our lives working. Yet, to most middle school students, being "grown up" is distant, especially for the sixth graders that I work with. Some of these students start the year at ten years old. In asking about future career plans, we are asking a question that is framed by an adult view of the world—an adult dream of a future where the child has a meaningful job. Like most things, this can be okay in moderation. We can't get stuck in a distant world where we see a class full of future veterinarians rather than 11-year-olds who love to snuggle with puppies.

Developing the heart and gut along with the head is an acknowledgment of the full humanity of our students. We are saying that we both care about who you are and the way you feel now *and* care about who you are becoming and who you will be someday in the future. In this way, as teachers, we are accustomed to working in this "between zone" of being and becoming.

Teaching for the heart means that we are asking our students to use all their senses, to consider their emotions as they walk in the world. We are asking students to also consider the hearts and emotions of other people—people who we know and those who we are still getting to know.

Teaching for the gut encourages students to stay in touch with their instincts, their intuition. The gut is the accumulated knowledge of our bodies. It can be difficult to explain or put the knowledge of our body into words. The knowledge of the gut requires us to kindle the connection between our physical being and the physical world.

When we teach like an organizer, we are helping students to develop their head, heart and gut. We are aiming to awaken the senses and provide experiences that open our students to the broader world. It is the belief of the teacher-as-organizer that exposure to these experiences will invite students to find their full selves and move with peers toward creating the community power needed to create a better world. One of the most essential experiences is to meet another person. The way to do this is through a one-on-one conversation, which will be discussed after trying out a couple of options for awakening your senses.

Try It Out: Awaken the Senses

Indoor Sound Tour

Provide your students with a map of the school. This can be available as a "fire-escape" plan in a main office. Ask them to think about the different levels of noise that they might hear around the school. Create a key for your map with a range of sound levels. For example, yellow is a quiet and whisper level sound, orange is a few people talking with an "inside voice" and red is over ten people talking with an outside voice. Tour your school and take notice of where you hear what levels of sound. Color in your map according to your key.

Reflection Questions: Were there any areas of the school that were quieter or louder than you thought they might be? If we observed an area for an entire day, would we hear the same sound levels and collect the same data? What does this tell us about where people might meet? Would you be able to recognize any of the areas on our map just by listening? Should any of the areas have different volume levels than what we observed? Do you have any recommendations for how we might use these data to create a better community at our school? How would you make these recommendations happen?

Notice that in the reflection questions, we are asking about the "way it is" and the "way it could be"—concluding with how we get there. Even if we don't use these data for our community in the "here and now", we are developing our ability to use our senses to be in the present and think about how we shape the future little by little. Doing a group activity like this can be a good bridge to one-on-one meetings between the students as it gives the students a common experience that they can talk about and reflect on together. The reflection questions can even be a good way to provide some structure to the one-on-ones.

(Adapted from Anderson, 2017)

Try It Out: Sensory Tour (Alternative or Extension to the Activity above)

When we think like an organizer, we should consider the wider range of relationships that we can create with the area where we teach and learn. It can be helpful to consider the model of civic ecology in this regard. Civic ecology is a model of viewing the people and places of the civic world as relationally connected, like a spiderweb of connection. Exploring nature or the physical world helps students to gain a tangible sense of a model of civic ecology. It shows students the way human systems mirror the natural world. A great way to start to explore civic ecology, as well as a great way to have students tune into their senses, is to use the animal sense activity below. This simple observational tool allows students to see, hear and feel the world through the perspective of animals. This is in line with one of the core principles of nature-based learning outlined by Sobel (2008). It's noteworthy that this activity can be done even if you don't have access to natural spaces.

Name:_____- Period:_____
Learning to Read the Land

Directions: Use the prompts below to use your senses and learn about the land.

Expanding our Senses	Notes + Ideas + Sketches
Owl Eyes: What do you see? Moving slowly and rotating around take in observations	
Deer Ears: What do you hear? Tune into the different sounds, wind, animals, humans, water, plants, machines, earth. Change the positions of your ears. Stand up or move close to the ground.	

Learning to read the land.

Racoon Touch:
Feel your feet on the ground. Feel the temperature of the air or wind on your face. Feel leaves crunch and crinkle. Feel bark and different textures.

Notes:_____

_____

_____

_____

(Cont.)

One-on-One Meeting

We have to know one another to trust one another. We have to trust one another to share ideas and take action with one another. Yet, where can we find the time to get to know one another? The one-on-one meeting is a method for students to get to know one another and also a way for teachers to get to know students. And it can take as few as 30 seconds to start!

There are a variety of purposes for the one-on-one meeting. The most essential thing in the classroom is to build relationships.

If we believe that we need interpersonal connections to have a strong community, then the slow and intentional building of relationships through one-on-one conversations is truly important.

The one-on-one conversation provides time for both participants to exchange ideas and express who they are as individuals. While person-to-person dynamics and the past experiences of individuals will influence conversations, the one-on-one conversation is a chance for seeing a person eye to eye at a point in time. We acknowledge that each person can change and that trust is built over time.

For students, I've found it best to start small when building the muscle for one-on-one conversations. We will have short conversations early on in the year. The conversations will range from 30 seconds to a minute and will often be on topics that are fun and easily accessible.

From that starting point, we can slowly mix up partners, increase time, try more challenging topics or have students create their own topics for one-on-one conversations. These conversations can be the focus of a larger lesson, a routine check-in after an activity or a way to reflect at the end of a class.

Assess and Meet about Our Conversations

Try It Out: Concentric Circles

Note: This activity can take as few as 3–5 minutes.

Ask students to create an inner circle and an outer circle. Students should face one another. Provide a short prompt for students to respond to and explain that the inner person will have 30 seconds to share their opinion, followed by their partner on the outer circle who will also have 30 seconds. State the prompt, count down 3–2–1 and start the 30-second timer. Let the groups know when 30 seconds is up. Restate the prompt, count 3–2–1 and start the timer for the outside circle partner. Once both partners have spoken, ask the students on the outer circle to rotate two partners clockwise. Repeat the process with the same or a different prompt.

Head, Heart and Gut

"Intuition does what intelligence never can: It brings us into the world as it is". — Henri Bergson.

Fostering the development of a holistic sense of self requires that we encourage students to reflect on one-on-one meetings and experiences more generally with the head, heart and gut. When we think about the classroom as part of public life, the head, heart and gut can be a helpful framework for reflecting on how our interactions with others are adding to a richer and more meaningful civic life. Part of a rich and meaningful civic life is a sense of commitment to one another and to the issues that we face collectively.

Encouraging students to use the head, heart and gut framework (below) to reflect and figure out the degree of interest and possible commitment that our partner(s) might have for a given issue, project or relationship can help us to build a sensitivity and consciousness to building commitment between one another.

Part of building sensitivity, consciousness and commitment is practicing empathy. It can be helpful to remind students that even in short one-on-one meetings with one another, we need to be respectful of ourselves and one another. This requires patience on the part of the teacher and the students as not all students have experience in practicing self-love or self-respect.

As teachers, we have witnessed students who lash out verbally or retreat inward when asked to talk with a partner for even 30 seconds. This can be isolating for the student with the negative response. It can be off-putting and confusing to the student who is initiating the conversation. For these reasons, it's helpful to discuss with students that the point of the initial meeting is to practice conversation and then to reflect. There is no "wrong" response. We just want to be considerate of one another and inviting. We can even tell students that we may ask to start a meeting with a peer and get an immediate response: negative pushback. The person might say, "I'm finishing a project". In that case, we can have tried and can move on to reflecting.

After the meeting, we can ask students to reflect on the meeting with their head, heart and gut.

Reflection questions:

Head—What did you ask? What did the person say?
Heart—What did the person say that connected with your passion?
Gut—What kind of energy would this person bring to a partnership?

Addressing Fear and Anxiety

Students have fear and anxiety. We all do. There are predictable times during the school year that anxiety and fear rear their heads: the start of school, leading up to breaks and the end of the year. These are the times of transition. Building community through providing a setting for intentional relational experiences can reduce anxiety and fear, creating a chance for students to feel known and to feel a sense belonging.

Community and belonging are salves for isolation, loneliness and fear of the unknown. And for many students, the transition times of the year are critical to establishing the clear benefits of our classroom as a community space of learning. If we can show students that the feelings that they feel in their bodies, like anxiety and fear, are natural—not something to suppress, we can show them how valuable it is to be part of the classroom community right from the start.

Anxiety has a way of creeping up on us. It may be one of the emotions that defines the current era in school. Perpetuated by the siren song that is social media and the buzzing, ringing and never-ending scrolling of our digital devices. It is a shadowy figure in classrooms, even in schools where devices are meant to stay away in backpacks and lockers. It's a lot for everyone. The fact that anxiety creating devices are almost inescapable makes our classrooms that much more important. The classroom can be a haven that takes students out of the hyper-individualized market-driven attention traps that are phones. We can be a break that disconnects students from social media and reconnect them to social learning.

Methods for reintegrating social learning spring from the physical world. The physical world recenters our rootedness to the grass, soil, concrete and wood chips around us, reducing anxiety by reminding us of our connection to place. Our bodies are telling our students and us through fatigued eyes, brain fog and anxiety that we need to go analogue—that we need to be in touch with the physical places we inhabit. That's why as teachers we need to prioritize time where students can gain the experience of being in the community, off the screen and outside.

Research on what has been called "Nature Deficit Disorder" (Louv, 2005) has demonstrated the adverse effects of our indoor, on-screen lives. These lives are split from so much of the history of human existence, severed from the natural relationships and myriads of health and well-being benefits that arise from being in relationship with the land and animals. As organizers we must use what we implicitly know to be true: humans, especially ones that are still growing, have a deep craving to be outdoors.

The frictionlessness of the online world presents challenges to the teacher-as-organizer who is working with young people accustomed to the ease of digital life. Confronting the anxiety that is produced from real-life social experiences in ways that are fun or through using predictable structures that add a sense of safety (like the activities mentioned above) can help ease "big feelings". At the same, one of the most valuable things that we can do is to provide room for students to display their feelings and to see that they can confront anxiety in a caring environment.

Anxiety has a way of shutting us down, it shrinks our world and reduces us to worrying about the future. In that worry, too many forget about the present moment—stripping away our agency, little by little. We are living through the effect of this on both a grand and a personal scale. The politics of worry damages our body politic because it incapacitates us and prevents us from using our civic muscles. Instead, civic muscles atrophy. Schools must adapt and provide the kind of civic exercise that helps students and our wider community escape the doom loop and get back on track.

Getting Back on Track by Welcoming

> "Being an organizer is tossing out the welcome mat."
> Ellen David Freedman

Scavenge to Build Social Connection

The start of the year is the perfect time to show students that we'll help them to learn what they really want to know. Let's ask ourselves, what is it that students want to know when they are entering our classrooms?

Yes, there will be the smattering of students who want to know if they can pick their own seats and how much homework will be assigned. In our middle school, the sixth graders that I teach want to know how to get around the school—practical knowledge.

In response to this, my colleague, a teacher for over two decades, Sean Curran, designed a scavenger hunt that takes students to all different corners of the school. Students work in teams of five to eight people. Each team of students receives a sheet with clues that must be completed in order. The teams start on different clues and each clue leads to a destination where a small envelope has been stashed away. Each envelope has a small paper puzzle piece in it. Once students have visited each location they rush back to our common area and put the puzzle

> pieces together to decode a secret message about our interdisciplinary team. It's a tried-and-true activity that gets the students excited, moving and talking to one another as they also gain practical knowledge in getting around our school. Games, like scavenger hunts, can bring students into the moment, reducing anxiety for many while also building social connections.
>
> **Reflection questions:** How are you feeling about being able to get around and find places in the school? Who was one person you talked with during the hunt? Who is one person you would like to talk to that you haven't yet spoken with?

Developing Our Civic Muscle with Others

Another layer of the one-on-one meeting is cultivating the civic imagination and exercising civic muscles. Civic imagination is something that cannot be developed individually in isolation. We need one another to share how we feel about our community if we are to rebuild and maintain it. The one-on-one conversation provides the time and structure for starting to see if others are driven by the same issues that we care about. The one-on-one meeting is the place where we can sense if people like things "as is" or if they would like to pursue change. The more conversations we have the easier it becomes for us to detect who is interested in what. When we know each other's interests, we have a better chance to create an agenda for growth in our community—or even within a class project.

It may be cliché, but change starts with you. It starts with each of us individually going and taking a moment to see where we are now, who we are now and who we are in community with at this point in our lives.

Get in touch with your authentic self and authentic teaching style NOW. Use your gut, heart and head (in that order) and figure out where you want to go and where you want to grow. Don't get caught up in the feeling that what you are now isn't enough. You are enough. The system as it exists now needs mending. We all have our ragged edges. We all need some mending. That system is the result of so many folks outside of the classroom, even many with good intentions, acting and shaping the reality inside the classroom both through policy and through culture. As people dedicated to the craft and art of teaching, this is our time to make things better. And we can't make things better if we feel depleted or defeated.

Developing our civic muscle means pushing ourselves to teach and learn in a manner that grows our democracy. Dewey (1916) famously wrote about the need for learning to be social and "associational". In other words, he saw value in the kind of learning that we do together. Democracy, in his view, wasn't knowing the three branches of government or the names of past presidents, it was defined by the actual activity that we do together, our commitment to being together and acting together. Now, you might learn about the branches of government through social activity, but that is rather supplemental, or perhaps even incidental to the main work of learning together. This approach is an invitation to all teachers to teach as organizers—to teach democratically. When we do, it strengthens people-powered democracy by providing students with not just one class, but classrooms everywhere that help to develop their civic muscles.

Teaching as an organizer, placing dialogic strategies like the one-on-one conversation in the center of learning, provides us with core methods that can be practiced and refined. These methods can also be transferred and applied to various content areas. Within the traditional concept of civics, core skills like advocacy, storytelling and mobilization can be honed through the lens of teaching as an organizer. Similarly, concepts of service-learning, place-based learning and civic engagement can be supported through teaching like an organizer (Anderson, 2017, p. 2).

Let's now look at why and how a community organizer uses the one-on-one meeting to start to "set the agenda" and create a team for positive change in the community.

Why and How Community Organizers Use the One-on-One (Examples from Teacher-to-Teacher Organizing)

Community organizers use the one-on-one meeting as a chance to build relationships. We find people who could share possible common interests with us and say, "Let's see if the interest is real. Does this person want to change? What are our shared values? Does this person want to build a relationship?".

All of these questions are in the mind of the organizer. Acting as a community organizer means that the one-on-one is not for the sole purpose of developing friendship. Friendship is great and it's a cornerstone of long-term civic health and collective action. But friendship alone does not create community. Friendship in large part can be in the zone of "private relationships". As teachers we live in the "public realm" meaning that we prioritize individual development with a heart for the public good. Shared purpose and values, as well as a commitment to working together to bring positive change, build community.

There are many people with whom you can be in relationship. But as humans we only have so much time. This means training yourself to get good at detecting the answers to the kind of community building questions mentioned above. Create the intent in your mind when you sit down with a colleague for a one-on-one conversation: this is a conversation to assess what and if we are going to take action together. Try to keep the conversation short, under 5–7 minutes. Get a feel for if there is potential for this to be a public relationship (you could take action toward bringing your shared values to life), if it might be a private relationship (woo-hoo, a new friend!), or just a polite acquaintance (that's okay—we will just keep doing our own things. You know the drill, give a polite smile and say, "Good Morning, can you believe it's only Tuesday?" when you see them at the copy machine).

Be in tune with your gut. Your gut will tell you which of three categories this conversation is falling into. Your head may try to rationalize the conversation and analyze the little nudges from the exchange. Your gut knows the answer. Will this person help? Yes. No. Or give it time to rest. It may sound a little harsh or judgy to take this approach. But it's even more harsh to waste your time and the time of others if there isn't the kind of relationship that you want to pursue there—or at least the potential for that kind of relationship.

You may get stuck in a conversation. I did. As an empathic listener, I wanted to hear all about what the person had to say. I thought that my listening and ethic of care would lead to a relationship of greater depth. That was a mistake. There are people who just want to vent—and you don't have time to be the person who holds everyone's emotional baggage. Again, it sounds harsh, which is why I tried to fight it; I was left feeling like I was running an emotional concierge service.

Instead, I could have been surfacing the relationships that give back. Whatever kind of change you want to bring about into the world, if you spend your time holding bags instead of holding space for conversations that generate change, then your mission is stalling out. Precious time is ticking away, and the forces of the status quo are entrenching their positions further.

Be kind to yourself. Learn from the mistakes I made. Learn from the mistakes you will make. And have shorter conversations that help you to assess the viability of public relationships. When we feel a sense of urgency about our work, that sense motivates us, yes even those of us with introverted tendencies, to move into action and use our time to start to gather "our people" together. It will take all of us to make the change happen, whatever that change may be.

Extending Our Practice: The Synergy of the One-on-One and the Small Group Meeting

It can be helpful to take a minute to think about what your change goal might be at this point. Organizers think about two types of synergistic meetings: the one-on-one meeting and the small group meeting. So far, we've discussed the one-on-one meeting. Working in a small town or a small school, sometimes you want to stick to one-on-ones. But as you grow your change goal outward, you will need to move toward a small group meeting. The goals of the one-on-one meeting are to test for a public relationship and to surface leads for small group meetings. One-on-one meetings that feel positive should end with a question that grows your connection and commitment to acting together. This can be an invitation to an upcoming small group meeting.

The small group meeting provides you with a forum to meet new (5-10) people, to share how you see the world and how you think the world should be with a larger audience. Again, we are all constrained by our limited time, so the small group meeting is a change-force multiplier. The goal of the small group meeting becomes to find who among the small group is a potential leader who you want to create a closer public relationship with—this is a person you want to have a one-on-one conversation with. The dynamic then starts to create a reproducible model where the new leader goes out and conducts their own one-on-one conversation that can lead to a small group, that can lead to another new leader and the branching out of the work, like an expansive root system of a tree. The helpful question to weave into one-on-one conversations is: do you know a few people who you could get together to talk about making this change happen? Let's schedule a time and date to do that.

Step into Public Life

As I previously mentioned, the one-on-one conversation is a step into public life. As teachers, we are familiar with aspects of public life. We've been told that upon signing a contract and stepping into the classroom that we are entering a "fishbowl" where all eyes are on us—especially in small towns and especially if we live in the small towns where we work.

Still, public life has a deeper meaning than the transactional exchange of services rendered (classes taught) for paid compensation. We grasp this intuitively as teachers. Surfacing the meaning of public life requires that we step into the public arena with a sense of agency, a sense that we can use our heads, hearts and guts for the purpose of improving the common good. Many try to do this alone. We fail when we do. That failure is a learning experience that reminds us that things are often accomplished at the speed of trust. Trust is created through shared values—which can be found through one-on-one conversations. Creating systemic change takes time, relationship building through conversation and trial and error on the part of the organizer. One-on-one conversations are the essential tool of starting to get things rolling.

Gut Test Example

On a sunny fall afternoon, I was preparing to referee a middle school soccer game. The two teams were finishing their warm-ups when an alarm sounded. It was the lockdown alarm alerting everyone on the school grounds to take cover. The two teams rushed to the woods that lined the field. There, we crouched and laid belly-to-the-ground, on high alert, scanning and searching for signs of what was going on. Everyone waited, hushed. Firetrucks rushed in, sirens blared. The first responders searched the grounds. Eventually, they gave the "all clear" signal. It had been a false alarm. Everyone was shaken by the experience and the game was canceled.

I share that story, because events like that have brought all kinds of teachers into public life–demanding that we take action to protect all our students from the scourge of gun violence. When I discuss this event with adults—and the fact that I see more courage from students who have staged walkouts than from our political leaders—I immediately get a gut sense of who believes we need to act for change. "Hey, that's just the way it is", some respond in our one-on-one conversation. That response is a message of that person isn't ready to act. That's okay. That person isn't a bad person. They just aren't ready now. It's our mission to find the people who are ready now. The urgency of "now" is something we feel in our gut.

It can feel like your gut is churning when you share your call to action with someone whom you respect and they give you a non-response. The non-response is a sign. The sign is "move on". Don't take it personally. It's not personal. It's a gift of time. Use the time to find people who are ready, who do want to act for change and who do want to help build something better with you, something that can help solve the pressing problems of today.

Building Social Connections with Families

Holding a paper and having something in your hand is a great way to build social connection. When we have something in our hands, we can give it to someone else—a gift! Or, at least it's a symbol of a gift. The true gift is social connection.

It can be easy to forget about the social aspect of physical objects in our digital age. An example of this is the anonymous digital survey. Digital surveys can be a great tool, no question about it, but when they are overused, they lose their effectiveness. When we are asked to take a survey providing feedback on a dental cleaning, on our purchase of toilet paper and to rate every meal out—there is a point where we feel over surveyed and there is a law of diminishing returns when it comes to continuing to ask for feedback. Digital surveys thrive because they are scalable. It's easy to send out an email blast to an entire group. It's pretty cheap too, both in terms of the time and the people needed to reach many potential contacts. But what if this kind of digital outreach (that happens in school too) is all wrong? What if it is missing the mark entirely?

Hold something in your hand that you can give out on open house night. It could be a small card or flyer with information about the upcoming book fair or soccer team tryouts. Handing that card or flyer out becomes an excuse to have a conversation, to have a contact point that can be the start of a relationship. We are welcoming, gifting and warming the space with our presence and openness.

It is also important to have a sign-in table where you ask for the names of the parents and family members who attend your open house (or any other school-related event). If you work with an interdisciplinary team, split up and have some people "work the room" talking with families and have at least one person at the sign-in table. If you are a solo teacher, set out a clipboard by the door to your classroom in a place that can't be missed and be sure to end every conversation by asking the family member to sign up. Ask for their best contact information. Ask them if there is something that they would potentially be excited to share with the class this year. Even if your school has a lot of this information in their digital system, it's important to make contact, to ask and to have your own list.

Be deliberate about posing a question that frames a positive outcome related to parent and family participation. This is an organizing move where you are asking the parent to visualize and start to articulate the hopes they have for getting involved. It doesn't have to be perfect. It's an invitation to think about contributing in a way that might otherwise not be asked about. We don't need to ask for a hard commitment at this point in time, it's merely the seed of a future conversation. Some folks may want to ask you about the question or may really have an idea of what they would like to contribute, that's all good. Take note of it. We know that families are also busy and have many commitments. Working lives can be full enough as is and we aren't trying to add more stress, obligations (or guilt) for anyone. We are just looking to invite and start to imagine what experiences might already be influencing and touching the lives of the families that we are learning alongside. Absent a hopeful, future-oriented question, we have one less foothold to build that hopeful future. Give yourself and your students that foothold.

We can use the foothold created by gathering family experiences to have conversations with our students. Initially, this can look like a follow-up conversation with each student. These conversations can happen when students are arriving for the day, when they're transitioning between subjects or classes, or during an advisory or homeroom time, if your school has one. These less formal settings are ideal for gauging student comfort level with the topics, their comfort with talking about family and their comfort in talking with you as a trusted adult. All this is helpful for us to determine whether and how to proceed with integrating families into the classroom. The student is the most important person in this relationship—and it's always important to remember to go at a pace that is comfortable for the students in these discussions. Some students will be excited to share or have family join the class. Others might be embarrassed, not have family members available or have other complicated homelife situations. The messiness of life is something that can deter some teachers from having these discussions. Start small. Try to use the information you gather to talk with students and see where they want to go with it, if anywhere. There are more ideas on how to connect learning to community in Chapter 5.

Creating and keeping your own list shows the adults in your students' lives that you are interested in connecting learning to the lives of your students. It gives you a chance to track who is coming to what event over the course of the year. This can allow you to assess how your communications and events are meeting the needs of the intended audience (the students and families). It also gives you backup contact information in the case of school records being incomplete or out of date. Record the interactions you have with families to consider how the knowledge, skills and stories of the families could support and be woven into the learning. You might be surprised about the opportunities that arise out of your work (more on this in Chapter 5).

Inquiry and Action

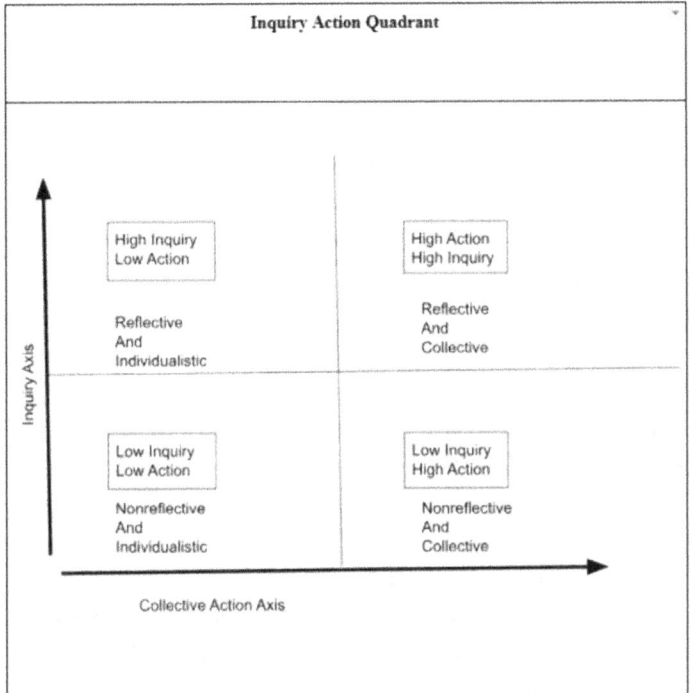

Inquiry action quadrant.

To this point, we have primarily been discussing how to use the one-on-one conversation as a tool of inquiry. By this, I mean that we are using inquiry to find out who our students and families are. We have encouraged students to try to have a one-on-one short conversation and help to create a feeling of social comfort in the emerging classroom community. Along the way, I've tried to emphasize the one-on-one conversation as tool to build relationships with people.

We have also thought about the one-on-one conversation in the context of the open house and starting to initiate organizing our families with the aim of including more family experiences in the classroom setting. All of this is good work in laying a foundation of care and trust among our people—the students and families. Our work here is to the point, we are expressing that we care and that our ethic is one of reciprocity, not one of being "an expert" who knows everything.

Time is a critical factor that determiners the actions we take in the classroom. It drives action by forcing us to prioritize what matters. Teaching like an organizer means prioritizing relationships. As teachers, these relationships are often time bound by the school year, but may extend depending on our situation (maybe we teach multiple grade levels, loop or continue mentoring or coaching students in capacities extending beyond the classroom). But since most of us have the constraints of the school year, we can think about what we might do together, as a classroom community.

For the teacher-as-organizer, what we can do is determined by who is in the room. The students that we have help us to determine what we can try. Their interests can help to guide us in creating classroom culture and learning opportunities. These things all start with the relationship, which is developed through one-on-ones. This isn't a one and done. We must cycle back and check in on how things are going. There will be highs and lows when it comes to exploration of self through inquiry.

When we teach like an organizer, we look for how our curriculum can provide a pathway for both individual and collective student action (more on this in Chapter 2). Along that path, it bears keeping track of how we are doing in terms of checking and continuing to build and maintain relationships through inquiry. Now, let's consider how all this inquiry can drive action.

A student learns to use a compass to navigate with peers and to learn more about the lay of physical land near the school.

The Inquiry, Collective Action Quadrants

The chart above is a tool to help us notice how relationships are developing within our classrooms. Since we believe that relationships are the foundation of learning and civic health, it's important that we have a tool for tracking activities and interactions that reinforce that foundation and that move us toward a stronger community. The frequency of what we observe in the classroom allows us to adjust instruction to help foster a space where relationships can take root and grow. It can also give us insight that we can use to structure our instruction going forward. The goal is always growth. Noticing how individuals grow, change and learn to work with one another is how we can help nurture growth.

The **low inquiry, low collective action** quadrant is where we observe more individual-based classroom activities. Mixing in individual practice or focused reading time can be an important part of learning. This quadrant is also where we might observe small groups of students learning to work together. As we know, the classroom is a place where interpersonal conflict can bubble up—and that's okay as long as our students are learning from it in a safe and productive manner. Interpersonal conflict can reduce inquiry. Notice that and respond. Help students to use questions to navigate the social environment of the classroom. Conflict can also drive down collective action. Low collective action can mean that students are taking action on an individual basis, but are not yet working together in a significant way. That's fine.

The **high inquiry, low collective action** quadrant is where we observe students starting to question one another and course material. Students ask inquisitive questions, participate in a variety of discussions and are interested in using dialogue as a tool for advancing their knowledge and skill (either consciously or subconsciously). This learning is focused on outcomes that relate primarily to the individual. An activity that "tunes into our senses" would be an example of high inquiry and low collective action. We are all getting to know ourselves, learning to trust our senses, but we are not yet working together. We reflect on what we learn to be able to move toward more collective action in the future.

Student tuning into his sense journaling.

The low inquiry, high collective action quadrant is where we observe non-reflective collective action. This looks like the group working together in a manner that does not question or make adjustments based on the lessons that are emerging from the learning process. As new details, truths and concepts come into play, this group has set its sights on an action and sticks to it. This quadrant can be helpful when groups need to make quick decisions, designate jobs and get jobs done. The scavenger hunt orientation activity is an early year activity that would fit into this quadrant. Students have to make quick decisions together about how to get around the school. They delegate who will read clues, collect puzzle pieces and take notes. The collective action in this case is low stakes but places the team on the path toward increasing their capacity for collaboration.

The high inquiry, high collective action quadrant is where we observe groups of students working together in a reflective process. They are integrating new information and supporting one another through dialogue to accomplish their commonly agreed upon goal. Each person has work that is meaningful to the overall group's goal. The group is tracking their own progress toward the given goal and making adjustments, if needed based on the information at hand. The result is a high functioning team that supports one another in a manner where everyone has an increased sense of commitment to the project because of the relational strength of the team members.

Actions and Reflections: The One-on-One Drives Growth

We call actions within the classroom: activities, lessons, protocols and sometimes we might use the fancy term "pedagogical moves". All these terms, and other similar descriptors, help us to identify what it is that we are doing alongside students to move together along the path of increasing our self-knowledge and collective capacity. Self-knowledge being our own personal awareness of our bodies, minds and hearts. Collective capacity being our connection to one another as humans and the wider ecological world—a connection that calls us to act together to protect, nurture and imagine a healthier place of co-existence and dignity for all.

Actions in themselves do not always "work", but there is always a lesson that we can draw from them. What I mean by this is that we can set up an activity with the intent that students will work together. That doesn't mean that the students will work together. They have their own agency. We, as teachers, can provide the opportunity for reflection that can lead to growth—yet again, the learner has agency. As the saying goes, "you can set the table, but that doesn't mean folks will eat". In each case, we look at where students are trending on the "Inquiry-Collective Action" quadrants. Looking for trends can be helpful as there isn't always time to reflect personally with a student each day.

Instead, bring your noticings to the time when you can meet and set up the next step.

The one-on-one conversation can be used in this context to help students to identify and move forward with their own goals, even when the student may be embedded within a small group. We have gathered our own observations about the student, and in the case that we have little to observe, we can listen to the student to explore how they are feeling about their progress and their learning. Listening in a non-judgmental manner is a core concept to teaching as an organizer. We want to invite students to participate in open self-expression.

Use the organizing conversation framework to generate questions that are pertinent to where your class is within the year and with reference to the stage of development of your relationship with students. The framework is flexible, but is essentially: What has been going well? What has been a challenge or what is getting in the way? How do we move forward? There are many iterations of this framework, and you can reorder the questions to work for you.

It is key that we remember to prioritize the relationship because there are many tricky aspects to the one-on-one conversation in the school context. Students can sometimes feel that withholding their participation or speech is the one thing that they can control. As a result, sometimes students don't want to have a one-on-one conversation. It's also possible that students are willing to talk about one of the questions but not the other questions—it is very likely the moving forward question can be the place where students get stuck. This question asks for students to take part ownership in their learning This can be an unfamiliar invitation for students that creates uncertainty.

For example, I have worked with teams where at the start of the class students are breaking up jobs to be completed and there is one student who doesn't want to communicate with the others. When asked by his peers which of two possible jobs he might like to take on with the group, the student doesn't respond. The other students pick their jobs and move forward with the work. In this case, our conversation (as the teacher) with the silent student isn't necessarily about getting the job done and catching him up completely to where his peers are. Instead, in my one-on-one, I tend to focus on how the silent student can communicate his needs. It may be that the silent student was concerned that once he had chosen a job that he would have to work side by side with the other students and that he was worried about being able to concentrate in such a close desk arrangement. When we discuss "how do we move forward?" We might make the plan that in the future once he picks a job he can move to a side counter where he can have more "think space". If we try that plan and he starts to communicate which job he would like with his peers but then doesn't get his job done at his alternative seat, then we can keep working on the problem—helping the student to learn how to learn.

The one-on-one conversation is a driver of growth that places us as teachers in direct dialogue with individual students. In doing so, we are sending implicit messages to the students about their value, about their agency and about what it means to be a part of a community. To grow is to be known. The one-on-one framework is a chance to figure things out together, it's not imposing the ideas of the adult on the student. As such, it models the respect that we need for one another in order to move from "low inquiry, low action" to asking questions about ourselves and our surroundings to working together and solving problems in a way that moves us further along the continuous path of learning to act together.

AEIOU: An Action Framework Based on the One-on-One

Learning to act together is all about testing things out and learning from how things go. There are many acronyms in the field of organizing, just like in the field of education. One acronym that helps organizers to frame their thinking about potential actions is "AEIOU", yes, just like the vowels. Here is what each of the letters stands for: A, Agitate, E, Educate, I, inoculate, O, organize and U, uplift. This short mnemonic can help to think about our purpose in one-on-one conversations that are oriented toward action. Agitation can help raise questions and concerns (more on this in Chapter 3). To use a conversation to educate means to think critically about the components of the problem and how to move toward fixing them. The term inoculate means to assuage fears through addressing the possible outcomes—communicating the possible bumps in the road and speaking about fears help to reduce the element of the unknown (oftentimes, fear of the unknown is worse than knowing the real possibilities or facing the real thing). Organizing in the context of the acronym means to help each person fit into a team role that best fits their talents, development and interests. Some teachers capture the sentiment of this with the saying—"Aces in their places" —get students working on the things that they love and are good at. Finally, uplifting is about reflecting on the lessons learned from acting together and celebrating the "wins". The AEIOU framework can be applied flexibly, although it is popularly applied in sequence. Starting with raising questions and ending with uplifting the lessons learned is a coherent model for inquiry in the classroom.

Start small in applying the framework and experiment. Organizer and author Ed Chambers reminds us, "… we work on small, winnable issues at first, to train our people and build credibility …" (2008, p. 40). In many cases, the students who you work with will be unfamiliar with learning in this style. You have the chance to introduce them to it. Starting small and building confidence in being able to talk to one another, and then moving toward taking action together takes time. Start with something of high interest to students and see how it goes. Be sure to ask the students what they think about thinking and learning in this way.

AEIOU Framework Triad Share

Note: Create teams of three for this dialogue activity.

I ask each team to decide who will be "partner number one", who will be "partner number 2" and who will be "partner number three". Once students have decided who will be which number, I'll inform them of the jobs. Partner number one will listen to the question that I pose and ask it to partner number two. Partner number two will have 30 seconds to answer partner number one. While partner one poses the question and partner two responds, it is critical that partner number three listens carefully. When the 30 seconds of talk time are up for partner number two, partner number three will summarize what partner number two said.

We will then rotate the roles to give everyone a chance to answer the question (you can also switch the question after each round). In round two, partner one becomes the speaker, partner two becomes the listener and summarizer and partner three becomes the question poser. In round three, everyone will switch to the role that they have not yet tried. Partner three is the question asker, partner one becomes the listener and summarizer, and partner two becomes the speaker.

Each time, it's an opportunity to practice listening with intent and to practice brevity in our communication.

Sample questions:
- A—What do you think about school lunch?
- E—Who makes the decisions about school lunch?
- I—Are their people who would be upset with the lunches being changed? Why?
- O—Who is one person we would need to talk to about the lunches? Could you do it?
- U—What went well in today's conversation? Were you able to answer all the questions?

Final reflection (if there is time)—Write down the best points you heard between you and your partners and be prepared to share them with the class.

AEIOU provides us with a model of what it may look like to take action by working together. We are starting to visualize what is and what could be when we talk about the scope of an action or unit in these terms. We start to see the possibility of a resolution. This can be helpful to a learner just as it is helpful for an athlete to visualize what he or she may do before taking to the court or field. Visualizing the difficulties that we anticipate and the possible resolution while remaining flexible to changes that can and may likely occur during the scope of our work together can give a calming sense to the work. There is a feeling that we can get through the bad and the difficult. The key is that we must be steady, calm and persistent.

Action involves RISK

> *Let it be said, once and for all that we do not mean fixing in advance a pattern of knowledge, skill and attitude to which we shall fit our young people. That is the goal and the method of the standardized education of the formal school and that we eschew.*
>
> (Rugg, p. 4)—Harold Rugg, Democracy and the Curriculum

It's safe to do what we have always done. Or, if you are new to teaching, it's safe to do what has been done at your school before. When you try something new, know that you are not alone—you're taking action with the people you share the classroom with, the students. Your new lesson, your new unit, your new icebreaker: All these things are actions, both large and small that can shape the dynamic of the classroom. All these actions give you and your students a chance to reflect on what it means to act together. Giving time and space to reflect on the icebreaker, the lesson or the unit are all a path toward learning together in a more meaningful way. But none of that happens without risk.

Teaching like an organizer is a risk. It's a risk because at its core it is democracy in action. It is a living and breathing form of democratic pedagogy. When practiced in a tiny amount, it leads us to wanting more. When practiced in full, it is the art of collaborative communal renewal. And the beauty is the fractal, or repeating framework, that is built on relationships—relationships of purpose and shared values.

As the Progressive Era professor and educational philosopher Harold Rugg suggests in the quote above, we need methodological fluidity to be fully responsive. To me, that means operating under a framework that is responsive to the needs of the students. I bring awareness to my teaching that I'm working within a public school system, and that system has certain parameters, certain non-negotiables. In that system, as it exists, there are core content grade-level requirements and there are standardized tests. And in the post-pandemic era, there appears to be once more a strong push for standardizing much more of the curriculum—and a looming shadow of the feared "teaching to the test" and "test prep" curriculum. To hold the words of Rugg in mind at the same time as we teachers are feeling the effects of centralization, standardization and the influence of corporations who seek to make money off our students' data and through selling the latest fad—well it can feel like just too much.

This is where thinking like an organizer can help us to a better frame of mind. We can remind ourselves that we are in the classroom for the students. We can remind ourselves of what true learning looks like, feels like and sounds like. We can remind ourselves that we are part of a multigenerations-long struggle for progressive education in schools. That the ebbs and flows of the progressive movement in schools have often tracked with the wider events of the country and world. As a colleague once said to me, "Everything you see in society—you'll see it in school. The school is a mirror of what's going on out there". We are not called to solve all the problems of the world, nor correct the entire system of public education, which we love despite its flaws, which we love because of all its promises. We are called to be with the students who we are working with now. In the present moment, we can reflect on the words of thinkers like Rugg and lean on the history of past colleagues, activists and caregivers who have come before us. We can find hope. And we can take the small step that leads to another small step that keeps us moving our students toward community. Nothing is promised. We get that. When public schools can feel like pressure cookers, we know that it's more important than ever to keep the vision of schools for everyone, schools that are for all kids—regardless of their parents' income or background.

Dare we take the risk of holding onto the hope that is a public school system that provides all students with the tools to transform our creaky, polarized democracy into a multiracial democracy where we can all be known, all be supported, all learn? Dare we teach like an organizer? When we do hold on to that hope, and show up in our classrooms, we can continue the slow and intentional work of creating learning spaces that are for the future—while honoring the present.

Group Dynamics and Structure

Class culture arises out of the long-term development of group dynamics. Group dynamics are built on individual relationships. If we are going to create a class culture that is a learning community responsive to the people in the room then we need to be able to keep an eye on both the micro-level of relationship building between students (and between ourselves and students) and we need to keep an eye on the macro-level culture that is developing as a result of the group dynamics over the course of units and throughout the duration of the year.

Students and adults bring all their lived experiences to the classroom—including our past experiences working with other people. Some of us naturally feel comfortable speaking to others and some of us are more reserved or prefer to process our thoughts through other means. Our comfort level, and the students' comfort level with different forms of dialogue and discussion, is a living thing. As such, when we treat dialogue development as living, which is core to relationship, group dynamics and culture, we think about how it may need to be supported in different times through varied methods.

Diagram #2 (shown below) is a helpful model for thinking about how we structure and support dialogue in the classroom. This model was introduced to me by Susan Dreyer Leon of Antioch University. The model shows that in cases where there is less social complexity there can be less structural support for dialogue. Social complexity could not only mean the number of people involved, but it also relates to social trust. When we have less relational history together, we have less shared experiences, and as a result the social complexity is potentially higher. It's potentially higher because there is a great deal of unknown. We may start to get to know each other and find shared interests, shared experiences or common friends. As our complexity (or the unknowns) increase, we as teachers, can add structural support to help our students through the complexity and the potential anxiety of the unknown.

Structural support can look like a protocol or routine. It can also be as simple as mixing up groups, changing group sizes or adjusting the duration of an activity. All these are tools for engagement and dialogue development. There is no predetermined "right way" when it comes to cultivating group dynamics. Instead, it is up to you to read the room. We all make the wrong (or less right) reading of the room at times. That's part of our learning process, part of us learning to apply the tools at our disposal with different groups of people who have different needs.

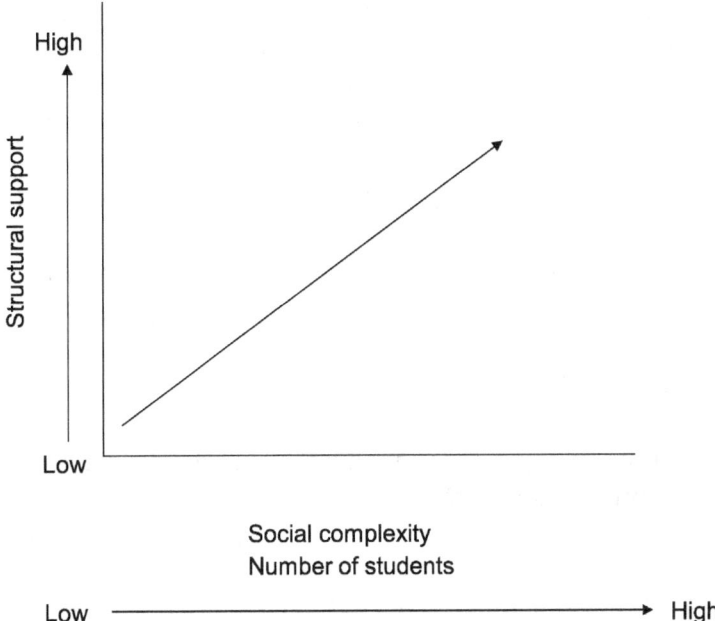

Structural supports and social complexity.

Our understanding of the relationship between social complexity and structural support can also guide us in making decisions when social complexity decreases. When we have shared experiences and have practiced routines, we may want to let go of the structures. Otherwise, the structures can start to feel like artificial barriers that inhibit relationships rather than supports that help us to build relationships. Keep observing when we do opt to let go of structures as social situations remain dynamic and it is possible that a new or different support could become practical. We want to be sure to model the kind of listening that students should be trying within the class or activity. That listening will give us clues about the next step to take. It can also provide the basis for a reflection with the class or a small group in the form of: "I was hearing _____". "What do you think the next step for us might be?" "Do we need to change something?" "What can we try that is different?" Questioning raises consciousness and invites students to initiate problem-solving that can renew the sense of purpose for the activity.

We cannot organize others if we don't organize ourselves! By this I mean we have to take inventory of where we are at with our various skills now, where we want to be and think of how we will get there. Each aspect of facilitating classroom life is a chance to run an organizing action on yourself. Pick one thing and do the work of getting a little bit better. Remember, don't get stuck on what went wrong—the lesson is your lesson. It's not a judgment on you as a teacher. Learn from it and move onward.

The Law of Change: Once in Motion

> "Everyday people need incremental success over months and sometimes years."
>
> Ed Chambers, p 80

Let's begin where we are, in the world as it is. Turn on the news. It's easy to get overwhelmed by the doom loop of the media. We are told every day about the environmental crisis, political crisis, bridges collapsing, cars crashing and a general fetishism of violence. It's overwhelming and maybe that's the point. When we are overwhelmed and fearful our instincts initiate the flight or fight modes. Neither avoidance nor aggression can help us to activate our civic imagination. Neither flight nor fight can help us to forge new relationships with people in public spaces. It's as if the news wants us to retreat from public space, wants to keep us isolated and wants to keep us separated. So, on second thought, turn off the news and tune into your lived reality.

We are heading in the right direction if turning off the news and deleting our apps is the first action we take. That's because we can start to once again tune into our bodies and hearts. We can start to have a mind that is clear. We can once again enter into public space without being mediated by an algorithm that is seeking to keep us on screen and away from public life. Public life means acting together and creating new relationships, and yes, even cultivating a sense of belonging from acting together. It affords us the chance to meet people with different views and experiences that we would not have run into in the mediated world of social media.

Years ago, Marshall McLuhan wrote, "The medium is the message" (1964). One of the messages of social media must be passivity. We sit and scroll and consume. Our attention is monetized. We are pacified. The public sphere shrinks. When public life shrinks, our civic life declines and our collective horizons are diminished. This is not to say that civic decline is solely the result of the media. Yet, it is a contributing factor to our present situation. It also helps us to see that there are other choices that are available to improve our current condition and reverse asocial trends that we all have been noticing and living.

In comparison, what is the message when the medium is a one-on-one conversation? The message is that you matter. While it may be uncommon for someone to seek you out, I want to know what you think. Whether we agree on everything is beyond the point—I want to know you. If we have enough shared will now, we can act together and have an even deeper relationship in the public sphere. If not, that's okay and we can be acquaintances or friends.

Think about the mysteries of the community where you live and the mysteries of the school where you teach. See the school through the eyes of kids, of learners. Walk the halls and take an inventory of what draws your interests. One of the first things that we can do in class with our students is to find mysteries and change those mysteries into deep knowledge of our human and physical community.

We have to wander and we have to explore new places—to try out new public relationships. Some relationships will take root and some may wither on the vine. But the act of trying, refining our practice, feeling how our body feels are all part of learning how to act publicly. We need to keep going once we start down this road. Just like the law of physics states "objects in motion stay in motion...", the teacher-as-organizer lives by the law "once in action will stay in action". You will find this law of organizing applies to the way that you act while teaching and it applies to the way you see your students in action in the classroom. Keep it going by knowing the friction points that can slow you and the class down.

Friction points and what to do

Friction point	What to do?
Students feel they "just can't do anything right" or "just don't get it"	Help explain the task in a succinct manner. If sentiment persists, consider decreasing the difficulty to provide the student with a "win". Build on the win going forward by celebrating it and finding the next logical "win".
Students are hesitant to ask questions to their peers in a routine dialogue	Provide a printed version of the questions that the student can refer to.
Students appear apathetic	Hold a one-on-one conversation to bring their feelings and passions to the surface.
Not all students in a group are doing their job	Assess if jobs need to be modified, switched or if a more extended consultation with an adult is needed.
Students want to take on an outsized portion of the project Example: Students want to change the entire school lunch menu	Find a small, related action. Try to help students break their big idea into smaller parts. Example: Have students invite the food service workers from the cafeteria to class Preview jobs for the class and consider assigning specific jobs to specific students to fit their needs, if they are not ready to make their own choices as a team.
Students appear fatigued	If possible, take a break from the day's work and take the time for a community building activity.

While we say, "students in action stay in action", friction can happen. It slows down the learning process. On the bright side, it can be a sign of possible growth. It tells us that learners could be approaching their zone of proximal development (Vygotsky, 1978). When things are easy, students glide along. When they reach a point where there is newness or novelty, there can be a learning curve. Friction can arise from encountering new skills, a new kind of interpersonal conflict or simply difficulty with understanding instructions for a new kind of process or problem. We can ask ourselves if this friction needs to be addressed by us (the teacher) or if it is something the students can work through themselves. If it is something that we feel like we need to intervene in, we can decide if there is a small tool that can applied to help the student to overcome being stuck, if there is a need to explore the issue through asking guiding questions or if the student needs some kind of physical change, such as taking a break or moving to a standing desk. These options, that teachers use every day, are also helpful to the larger growth model of the inquiry collective action quadrant (Diagram 1) and helping the student to move toward exploring deeper questions and taking increasingly collective action.

It's also helpful to remember that we and our students need to see "wins" over time. We are building a new culture of civic participation. This takes time, and to be sustained over time we all need to see that we're moving in the right direction. As you think about planning your units, consider the possible points where students might gain a sense of accomplishment. A small thing that can help groups is keeping track of their actions on a list, checking off completed tasks and having time to share out at the end of the class what they were able to accomplish. Alternatively, some like to have a "win board" or "leader board" where students can post sticky notes of their wins or track progress visibly through other means.

We can also acknowledge that students, like all people, act out of self-interest (at least some do some of the time). This doesn't mean they are being selfish. But it does provide a window into how competition can be motivating for students. Use competition to motivate those students who need help feeling like they have something at stake in the learning. Operate in the world as it is with students. Meet them where they are in their motivation and learning. You open the chance of moving the student ahead when you act on what you see rather than staying stuck in a "world as it should be" based on an inflexible philosophical position. Hook the student on earning and once they're hooked and acting, keep them acting.

Look out for Leaders

Each activity that we do in class is an opportunity to find leaders. The number one job of the teacher-as-organizer is to find leaders who can help the classroom reach its highest peak of learning. Leaders are not always the students who are the most talkative or the quickest to raise their hands. There are many times that I can think of the most talkative student in class needing to practice listening to enhance their understanding of peers. Without listening and understanding, the basis for peer-to-peer respect is eroded. Leaders are the students who gain the respect of their peers through being reliable, thoughtful and open-minded. Students of all different dispositions and experiences can be the leaders we need—in fact, our aim should be to develop the leadership capacity of every student. This will be further touched on in Chapter 4.

Between You and Me—Us: Dialogue and Pluralism

Public schools are the heartbeat of democracy. Our public schools bring together students of all backgrounds and beliefs to learn with one another and from one another. The idea that someone who was born into great privilege could learn from someone who was not is as democratic a notion as you can find. It is from this belief in people that our hope for changing our world for the better is constantly renewed.

But the existence of the public school isn't enough. We know that many public schools are under-resourced, underfunded and understaffed. We know that the kinds of stratification and segregation that persist in our society are often reflected in schools. And for these reasons, we must do the work of organizing for community and public power.

Organizing for community—for a public space of pluralism—means creating space for conflict. Working through conflict is how we forge community and build trust. It shows students that we have a process for talking about difficult things and it takes practice to learn how to sustain the kind of dialogue we need to keep a community going.

At the classroom level, the trust that we generate through clear processes for dialogue is a foundation for the school as a civic institution. Students can see that the institution—through teachers and fellow students—is responding to their problems and needs. Institutional faith is built through responding to the issues of the students in a structured and predictable manner.

Providing a process and structure for responding to student issues doesn't mean that students get whatever they want. We agree to listen to one another and help each person to be heard. To do this, we also agree that there likely will be opposite views and ideas. The varied needs of the individuals in the classroom community guide us to the understanding that we will need to occupy a space of compromise and discomfort in our class at times.

"Don't Give up when You Hit that First Bump"
—Ed Chambers

There are going to be bumps in the road. That we can guarantee. Don't give up. Sure, you don't know exactly what the bumps will be, but you know there is something coming. It can be easy to get caught up in the anxiety of what could go wrong. But, try to let that go. A big part of teaching like an organizer is letting go of what you can't control. It's like being on stage. You've put in the work, you know your lines, now go out there and do what you know how to do. The knowledge that something might go a little differently than you planned is a form of inoculation.

A Word on Reciprocity

One of the greatest models that we can provide in conversation with our students is our own story. Our questions alone will take us only so far. In fact, we should be prepared for students to "turn the tables" on us in this work—they'll ask us questions and look for us to share our stories. If they do, it shows us that they are learning new skills and feel comfortable enough to ask us about our lives and experiences. In my experience, students in one-on-one situations will ask you what you think, who you are and why you have come to the conclusions that you have come to. The same can be said about the adults you work with and the parents that you connect with. Each relational meeting is a chance to know someone else, to know yourself and to be known. Be prepared to share about yourself in a manner that conveys your own personal authenticity. Otherwise, it can be deflating to be on the verge of a meaningful conversation only to deny your conversational partner a level of reciprocity.

Conclusion

The public sphere is where we learn to act. Public school, as a site of community and as a site of the physical manifestation of the hopes of the adult community for the young, is a place for students to grow into public life. Public life is where we learn to act together through asking questions, listening, observing and reflecting on our shared work. Beginning to build a community of learners requires that we tune into all our senses and learn to think with not just our head, but also with our heart and gut. In so doing, we invite students to build a holistic knowledge of self and of others. Given the amount of distraction in our culture at large and the specific tools of distraction aimed at young people (phones, apps, etc.), it can be challenging to tune into our senses. But tuning into our senses is the building block for acting together and building a public and intentional community.

Student taking observational notes under the trees.

The one-on-one conversation is a vehicle for learning how to live together. It reaffirms our commitment to the "small d" democratic principle of honoring the individual. It brings us into conversation with those who are different from ourselves and allows us to practice pluralism—a salve for the festering wound that is our current political discourse. Entering into conversation at the individual level allows us to search for our commonalities, to share our interests and to be known.

Coming into relationships with others by definition enters us into the realm of conflict and friction. The teacher-as-organizer understands this and is ready for the "first bump in the road". Not only that, but we are also thinking in terms of the moves that we can make to help students along the road toward asking more questions and learning the power of acting together. We understand that our methods feel "risky" to some who might prefer neat rows and silent compliance, yet for us, we know that without the risk there is no reward—and the reward is a community of learners who are developing their civic muscles. As Ed Chambers reminds us, "We have to be willing to fail, and that takes courage" (2008, p. 32).

Finding common ground starts with being rooted in community.

Works cited

Anderson, S. K. (2017). *Bringing school to life*. Rowman & Littlefield.
Chambers, E. T. (2008). *The body trumps the brain*. ACTA Publications.
Chambers, E. T. (2010). *Action creates public life*. ACTA Publications.
Counts, G. (1932). *Dare the school build a new social order?* The John Day Company.

Dewey, J. (1916). *Democracy and education: An introduction to the philosophy of education*. Free Press.

Horton, M., & Freire, P. (1990). *We make the road by walking: Conversations on education and social change*. Temple University Press.

Louv, R. (2005). *Last child in the woods*. Algonquin Books of Chapel Hill.

Mcluhan, M. (1964). *Understanding media: The extensions of man*. Gingko Press.

Rugg, H. O. (1939). *Democracy and the curriculum*. D. Appleton Century Company.

Sobel, D. (2008). *Childhood and nature: Design principles for educators*. Stenhouse Publishers.

Vygotsky, L. S. (1978). *Mind in society: The development of higher psychological processes*. Harvard University Press.

Young, J., Haas, E., Mcgown, E., & Louv, R. (2016). *Coyote's guide to connecting with nature*. Owllink Media.

2

People before Program

How Starting with Place Helps Make Change Pocket Sized

My parents broke up when I was in sixth grade. My dad moved into an apartment above his shop and my mom spent a summer living in the hayloft of my grandparent's barn. I still remember looking back at our house in the rearview mirror as we drove away, longing for the life that I wasn't getting back.

That's when I met Mr. Dowling. It was his first year of teaching, but he came to the classroom after a lifetime of experience that included military service, carpentry and running. His classroom became my home away from home. It was a place where I could escape into the Greek myths—climb to the heights of Mount Olympus and descend to the depths of Hades. He invited me to use my imagination to write stories about spy adventures where I cast all my classmates into roles, sharing our most recent exploits during a weekly read aloud. Hearing their laughter and fielding questions from adults and my friends taught me something: school was where I belonged. Mr. Dowling also taught me that teachers are my people.

Issues become clear once we know our people. Our time living together, weathering reality and tightly grasping fleeting memories bind us together. As a teacher, I've found that the issues that are important to our experiences in the classroom are inextricably linked to the issues of the students. We know the frustrations of sticky locks and jammed lockers, of the awkwardness of not knowing where to sit in the cafeteria and the need for a friend who shares our interests.

People before Program

The saying "people before program" comes from the need to think about who we are working alongside. As teachers, this is our class and it is also the parents and caregivers. There is a curriculum (program) that we need to cover, but the coverage of that curriculum will not matter much if we don't understand the people who are along for the learning with us.

Another way to think about the mantra "people before program" is that we need to develop a stance as educators that asks us to check back in with our learners throughout the learning process—yes to see how the learning is going, but more importantly to see how the people are doing. It won't matter what we teach if we lose touch with the students.

"History is the most difficult subject", a professional development coach once told me, "because there is more and more of it to cover each year". The concept of "people before program" is the antithesis of this notion. Amid all the pressure to rush from one initiative to another, remember it is a profound act of respect to the humanity of the people who you spend your time with to place "people before program".

Developing a program also requires that we know the people and their wants, wishes and dreams. As teachers, we are listening to the students to try to determine the lived experiences in the room, the senses of humor in the room and the things that are close to the hearts of the students in the room. When we approach the classroom with a mindset of an organizer, we are thinking about present and future ways that we can create the program that fits with our group of students.

Getting Started

Each year, we are assigned a group of people to work with: colleagues and students, parents and caregivers. We slowly find out about one another, our backgrounds, experiences and dreams over the course of the first few weeks of school—and then continuously throughout the year.

For years, I have collected magazines from my local library in a big cardboard box. These magazines span the gamut in terms of topics. In the first few weeks of school, I invite students to page through the pile and dig deep into that enormous cardboard box to search for images that connect to them and their lives. Each student takes their selected images to create a collage on the cover of their classroom journal and they explain their choices as well as respond to a smorgasbord of questions about themselves. This is just one way to get to know my students a little bit.

And while they are ripping and tearing, uncapping previously pristine glue sticks to smother tiny bits of paper in what has become a start of the school year rite of passage—I'm talking to them about it all. I want to find their stories, find what they think is fun and funny. Find where they have been and where they want to go. The jibbitz on their crocs can give us more clues—and like a detective, we teachers are finding out who likes Angry Birds and who plays Mario, who loves trains and who is a self-styled bookworm. It's one of the great adventures of teaching to find out who our students really are, especially as the students are also finding out who they really are.

Deep and Relational Organizing

The terms deep organizing and relational organizing have shown up more and more as a reaction to the click-bait activism and online drives calling for participation through shallow forms of engagement. Teachers know instinctively that learning is all about relationships. But at the same time, we are awash with technological answers and tools that we both have become accustomed to using and that we are sometimes required to use.

The point of this section is not to create a binary of good/bad when it comes to tech tools and creating relationships in the classroom. Instead, we need to think about healing our communities by centering long-term relationship building. This means fostering a sense of belonging in the classroom and it means continuing the conversation about who we are and what we want to be throughout the year through informal conversations and through academic work and routines. It's through this ongoing dialogue that starts at the beginning of the year with icebreakers, collages and "getting to know you" kinds of assignments and continues forward earnestly with sincerity. Otherwise, it's a "one and done" kind of thing that can build cynicism. And teaching like an organizer is about taking down the temperature in our classrooms and communities—thinking about how we can foster the kind of relationships that day in and day out show that each person in our learning community matters.

Listening for Understanding

Community building is slow work. And it's more important than ever in the current post-pandemic polarized environment. Kids need someone to listen to them and they need to see that they have a place in the school community. We, as community building teachers, give students that space to belong to our school community. We recognize students for their talents and accept them for being who they are as individuals with families, histories and diverse backgrounds.

This groundwork must be our educational stance as we work together. It is part of everything we do and it must start long before we get into the "tough stuff". That's because this kind of intense listening with intentionality is at the core of the trust we have in one another. Affirming our trust in one another is the first step toward expanding our trust in one another. We cannot expand, scale up or grow outward without affirming our faith in one another and continuously checking back in on one another.

Our patience as teachers allows for us to develop these individual and communal bonds. It is in developing the practice of listening for understanding that we follow the 80/20 rule (listening 80% of the time and speaking 20%). In so doing, the teacher-as-organizer creates the space for students to have trust in the teacher and trust in their peers. This is the type of trust that allows students to start to express how they see the "world as it is" and start to be able to dream together of the "world as it could be".

Going Further: Gazetteer for Good

Teaching like an organizer means that we need to know the lay of the land, both the social landscape and the physical landscape of our community. We want to know the connections that students have to one another and the connections between students and families. This is important social knowledge that can help us learn more about the world around us and help us to contextualize learning for students. In my own practice, I've wondered: How could we express this work in an academic form? Answering this question has led me to play around with the idea of using mapping as a community affirming project—weaving a living form of geography into the classroom.

We start small. Students use their hands as units of measurement and create a space of five hands by five hands in an outdoor area by the school. Inside the 5 × 5 grids, students need to construct their own mini-community. This means creating little houses, roads, forests and landmarks. Students then map out their mini-villages on paper and explain how to navigate between different points of interest using relative location and also using the grid systems. Some kids like to bring extra materials from home. One girl brought in a bunch of small plastic minions to make "minion-ville", but most students use all natural materials or "found" materials that they can repurpose in their tiny towns. One all-natural village was founded in a soft bed of green moss. The student who created it dubbed it "Mossington, DC".

Student creates a mini-village using natural materials.

You could fit your arms around the amount of land that we focus on for this project. And that's saying something! By zooming in on the little details that makes a place special and defines it as unique, we are training ourselves to notice details, to think creatively about our use of natural and man-made resources, and to think about small-scale community building (literally).

This project is a small and simple example of where we can start when it comes to organizing for reclaiming common ground in our communities. With so many students spending significant time on screens in a world untether to the local environment, we are choosing to spend time outside getting to know the land. Our community space is not a sterile screen that could be "Anywhere, USA". It's not the Sims or iCivics. The significance of spending time with students getting to know the particularities of our own community, our own landscape, is that this is the place we live.

Using our time to dig into the richness that exists in our community tells students that it's worthwhile, that each of their own experiences is worthwhile. Using natural materials, thinking about the agency that comes with making something on your own, learning how to recognize and navigate the world in your own words, all reinforce the mindset that we each see our community in different ways and we each construct our ideas of community differently.

Still, we have so much in common and so much to learn from one another. There is always the moment when students look around and see the awesome mini-villages that their peers have made and they begin to borrow ideas and innovate from their initial designs. It's those moments that remind us all that we need to keep listening, we need to remain connected to one another so that we can keep growing.

We scale this project up throughout the year, adding different elements to our understanding of community, practicing learning from one another. We map out greater areas around our school, adding to our knowledge of the human and physical landscape. In doing this work, we see the world as it is and we can't help but to imagine things being a little bit different. When you teach like an organizer, this is the seed of change waiting to be watered and nurtured into civic renewal.

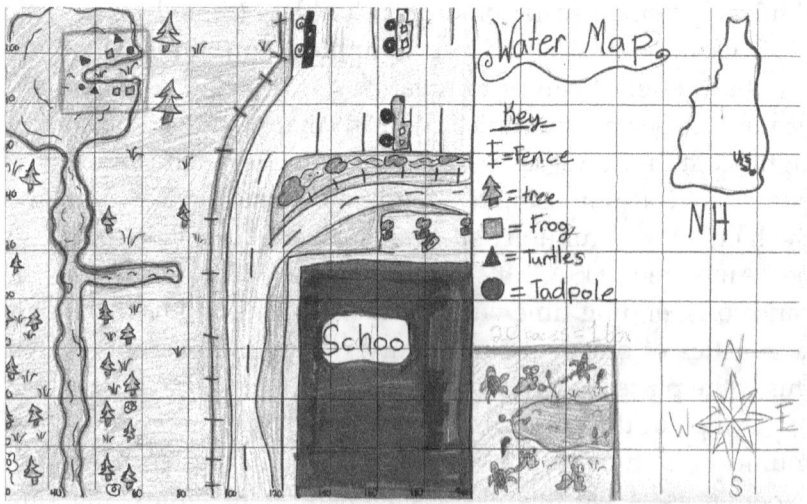

Student made map of our school grounds.

Try it Out: Tree Ring Tool

Teaching and organizing is about helping people to express and grow their inner goodness. In the classroom, we are under immense pressure to measure, measure, measure—this simple tool helps us get a quick read on how learners are feeling about a topic, skill or issue.

Draw three concentric circles on a white board. Explain that the diagram represents tree rings. The smallest ring in the center is known as the heartwood of the tree. Each year, a tree adds another ring. The tree may grow faster or slower depending on many different factors, including environmental conditions.

For our classroom purposes, the inner heartwood zone represents that space where we feel like we can teach others about the topic, skill or issue—we have the confidence and want to help lead.

The next circle out from the heartwood zone is the space for those who feel like they are solidly independent with a skill, topic or issue.

The third and final ring space is for learners who would like some coaching on the topic, issue or skill.

When you feel that you have a solid community in class, you can introduce this tool to learners. You might consider scaffolding this tool in to build more trust. First, have students self-assess on a paper copy that is just for them (no pressure to share). Later, when learners are confident in the concept of the tool, post the visual on a white board or bulletin board in class and provide sticky notes to students. Each student can write their name on a sticky note and place it where they would like—knowing that they can move between the zones at any time.

This tool allows students to self-organize and self-identify leaders within the classroom for any topic. Be on the look for ways to invite the diverse talents into the room over the course of the year to allow everyone a chance to shine as part of the classroom's "heartwood".

> Variation: If you want to get learners moving around, you can create three circles with jump ropes. You can read statements about an issue, skill or topic and get a quick gauge of how students are feeling before or after a lesson. Students move to stand on the part of the circles that reflects how they feel.

Natural Leaders

When we look around our classroom, we see natural leaders. These are the learners who other learners look up to and have already developed social skills that allow for fostering connection and community building. As a teacher-as-organizer, we see the potential for every learner to be a leader and also recognize that there is a long path to leadership that we each walk. Recognizing our natural leaders can help those young people to feel seen and encourage them to continue to progress down their own path. Sometimes the natural leaders are students who may struggle academically, but are on the cusp of being able to use their social skills for the common good of the learning community. The teacher-as-organizer is always on the lookout for leaders and is always thinking of ways that the leaders can take the next step toward being in the "heartwood".

How Does Place-Based Learning Help Us to Understand Our People?

Understanding people requires that we seek to understand their context, their place. In my sixth grade geography class, we talk about "place" meaning a couple of different things. One of the things that place means is the physical world: the mountains, hills, rivers, oceans, bays, etc. The other big thing that place can encompass is the human characteristics: culture, language and social practices. In my view, these definitions don't mean a whole lot to the students, but they are a reference that students can use for analysis, something that can help them think critically about the relationship between humans and the physical world. Hopefully, something that can help them think critically about their own relationship with nature.

Place-based learning is an approach to teaching that helps us to facilitate critical thinking about the human-nature relationship. Scholar David Sobel (2004), a long-time leader in the field of place-based learning, has defined place-based learning as initiating learning using the local community or environment. I love this definition because it's an invitation to look around our area and to get started. We don't have to do everything all at once, we simply need to find a point of entry, something that is fascinating about local life, something that is a place to begin to ask questions and wonder.

Making the place we live the topic of study tells us that the place matters, that we matter. Many of our communities are seen through the prism of what if anything can be extracted from them. The extraction may be natural resources, crops, or it may be leveraging the landscape to bring tourist dollars into the economy. All these issues are topics of potential study, but the issues alone, without exploration, can lead to a devaluing of the places where we live. We, our students and our community, are more valuable than money. The richness of our stories and our histories deserve to be honored and treasured and told. Place-based learning is an acknowledgment of this.

Studying place puts learning and the learner in context. Our experiences and histories are both unique to our time and place while also containing truths that are universal to the human condition. Examining the land where we live reminds us that just by being who we are where we are that we are connected to the past. We are connected to one another. This becomes apparent through place-based learning first at a proximal distance—we realize our connection to those who are closest to us. Our class starts to see the shared experience that they have today. Then students start to expand that sense of connection in all directions: into the past and into the present day at greater distances.

Start learning where you are, Sobel's advice on initiating place-based learning orients us in the direction of action. We don't always have a place to take action when we are learning about the big problems of the world, and that's immobilizing. By starting close to home with experiences that are tangible, we can still talk and research an issue with depth, but at the same time, we can be anchored by the common thread of what we have shared together in person, in our community. In this way, we are reminded time and again to find that thread and follow it back to a place where we can do work—where we can make a difference.

Place-based learning is not limited to rural settings. It is not limited to only natural settings. There are many examples of place-based learning taking place in urban and suburban settings. Sarah Anderson writes of many examples in her school in Portland, Oregon. In one example, she describes how students dug into local civil rights history, traveling to different landmarks within the city while learning about national events from the movement that connected to the local landmarks. From Portland, Oregon to Portland, Maine (example below) and everywhere in between, there are rich investigations that can engage students in gaining a better understanding of our communities just waiting to begin. Many of these studies relate to issues that your students have background knowledge of. They may be about things that they have always been curious about but never had the time to look into. The key is to consider the issues that are ongoing in your community—which may present case studies for students.

Gears of Power: Place-Based in a Small City

One teacher in Portland, Maine, who was a bike enthusiast, told me about a unit that he designed called the "gears of power". His students had said to him how they wanted to learn about green transportation issues—so he brought his bike to class. Using his bike as a metaphor for the change process, he asked the students what they noticed about how the bike functioned. "There's a frame", one student pointed out. "There are gears and the chain", another added. "How about the pedals?" another suggested. "But, you drive it forward with your pedalling and you steer it with the handlebars", the teacher reminded the students. "I want you to consider how we make change here in Portland in this unit. As you do, explain how each element of change relates back to the bike".

The class went on to research different modes of public transportation. They looked into the various inputs and outcomes, comparing the options that the city might have in adopting more green forms of transportation. Some even suggested adding more bike lanes as a possible solution. Before the unit concluded, the class took a field trip biking around town, visiting the various sites of local decision-making, including a stop to talk with officials at City Hall.

We keep our eyes open, like advanced scouts in sports, looking for the people and issues that may spark our students' interest. This way, we can learn more about the issues, learn the people and the language of issues, and prepare ourselves for possible paths that student learning may take. What I've found is that scouting issues in this way is a recursive process. We make contact with people and find issues, discussing ideas out in the community. We mull the feasibility of bringing ideas back to our classroom, we wait for student interest to develop or for circumstances to shift, and then we, as teachers, move into action, drawing on past conversations and rehashed units to co-create something that resonates with the students of our class. That is the hope in the active mind of the teacher-as-organizer.

How Is Place-Based Learning Relational?

It can feel like we need to rush our teaching. Each day, there is the rush to get things ready, to have classroom materials assembled, the papers printed and to then start and end each lesson on time. There is also the rush to change our practice, almost at breakneck speed. We are told that it's time to go in this direction, adopt this new curriculum, etc. It's reminiscent of a children's book by Kate Dopirak and Christopher Silas (2020) called *Hurry Up* that I read with my daughter. The main character realizes that they are rushing everywhere all the time and instead need to STOP. The "STOP" page is one of my daughter's favorites because it has a full page of red with the white letter STOP. Once the main character of the book stops, she looks around to see how amazing the world really is and how fun it is to be with her dog and friends. While of course it's good to be prepared for our lessons, much of this rushing is synthetic pressure that we are putting on ourselves and transferring (albeit often unintentionally) to our students. The author, adrienne marie brown (2017), suggests that we need less time on "prep" and more time on "presence". This mindset can help us decrease the anxiety that compulsively drives our thoughts and keeps us occupied.

Remember, when we teach like an organizer, we must be rooted in the world as it is—and the occupation of our mind with hurrying toward the future is a distraction from the here and now. It's a distraction from the real needs of our community, our specific place in the world. Starting to ease more presence and less prep into our lives as teachers is a reclamation of relationality. Conversely, it doesn't matter how prepared we are if the relationships in the room are not right. When we make the decision to prioritize this place, the location of your school and community, you are standing for the agency of everyday people. That is the work of the teacher as organizer.

As teachers and people who have the intention of using our time on the earth to help others become the best versions of themselves, that is to help others learn to help others, we must keep pace in mind. When we establish the pace of our work as being relational, we take a step back from rushing. From the perspective of teaching as an organizer, when we see the pace of our work as being shaped by the time-bound nature of teaching, we see that we need to be able to "zoom in" and "zoom out" of our fixation on time. At times, we need urgency to motivate and move us. We can call these the "zoom in" times—where we are focusing on the detail of the moment to meet the needs of people in this specific time. But it seems that with so many pressures around teaching today, we just as importantly need to be able to "zoom out". What I would like to propose is that "zooming out" is our ability to take the long-range view on our work in school and our efforts at building community. The long range tells us that if we remain hyper-focused and stuck in an "infinite scroll" of "next, next, next". We will lose our ability to bring our full selves to the work of educating our students. Keeping in mind the tools of the microscope (zooming in) and the binoculars (zooming out) we can maintain the perspective that allows us to be in control of the pace of our lives, our work and educational practice.

 Again, because our current condition is so heavily oriented toward the future and toward keeping us cognitively overloaded and overstimulated, I want to emphasize the critical role of place-based education in this time. Place-based learning places the tools for determining pace back in our hands as the educator. We know our community and students better than anyone else. Our experience teaches us the right time to slow things down in the classroom and when to take the long view—when to work on relationships. Ecologist David Orr has suggested that to know a place, we need to live in it through all the seasons, to see the sunrise and sunset in each season and to come into relationship with the land (2004, p. 213). Take comfort in the rhythm of coming into relationship with the land. There is an ebb and flow. Each day has a sunrise and a sunset. The teacher in us can organize to this beat, if we listen.

How Can You Integrate Place-Based Organizing into an Established Curriculum?

What Makes This Place Special?

Part of the sixth grade curriculum at my school has been the study of Australia. It's generally a topic in the first half of the year. Since there are many different approaches to teaching about an entire continent with 50,000+ years of human history and countless geographic features, it seemed worthwhile to try to relate our learning to the concept of place.

Rather than starting the study by broaching the topic of Australia, we went outside. There, we imagined if different natural features of the land around us could see, hear and feel, what they would be able to describe from being in that place for a day, season, year or decades.

As the last Beech Tree leaves clung to the branches, shivering in the late autumn wind, students sat under them, writing rough drafts of this imaginative work. Then we followed up by redrafting the work, which turned into short narratives and creative poems. The idea that we can use our senses in an everyday setting to reveal things that had previously been passed by or taken for granted is an immensely powerful tool. It's a window into the creativity that we can tap into with our students when we take the time to notice and observe in everyday places.

It also gives us a chance to think about other folks who are using their senses every day in communities outside our immediate vicinity. In the case of my class, the grade-level expectation was that we studied the continent of Australia. The sensory exercise allowed us to connect with and gain a deeper appreciation of descriptions of the land of Australia that had previously been left out of the curriculum. One such description was provided by Bob Randall, an Aboriginal man who lived close to the iconic red-rock monolith Uluru (Ayers Rock). Randall explained his deep connection to the place where he grew up and how he saw the land as "a library"—which led me to ask

Student artwork connecting to place by showing a constellation.

students, "if the land is a library, how do we learn how to read it?"

And in this manner, we wove back and forth between the local and immediate and communities far away that have similar questions and experiences relating to place. In so doing, we dug into this truth: the far away is in the immediate and the immediate is in the far away.

When we awaken our senses, we can tap into the knowledge that is all around us. This is a knowledge that is only accessible through direct experience. When we give the space for students to explore, to process and to develop their voices (and writing) in a way that underscores the vast power of our senses and our common humanity, we open the door to the kind of learning that can spark true creativity and a deeper sense of belonging.

Piece by piece, our class constructed a short book of poems, descriptions of places that have deep meaning to everyday people far away and creative writing about the land by our school that helped to answer our big question: What makes this place special?

While the books of the land that we created collected our insights, our questions are as important as what we uncover in our explorations. We are reminded that we are always finding new things about our special places. This mirrors our development as people who are discovering with each day new things about ourselves that make us special. Linking personal development with our understanding of place gives depth to our relationship with ourselves, with one another and with the land.

Becoming known through direct experience with the land, through writing and surfacing our own connection to the land teaches us more about our deep humanity and interconnectedness. We recenter learning in a way that promotes connection, reducing dissonance between at home and school life and builds positive relationships with the environment.

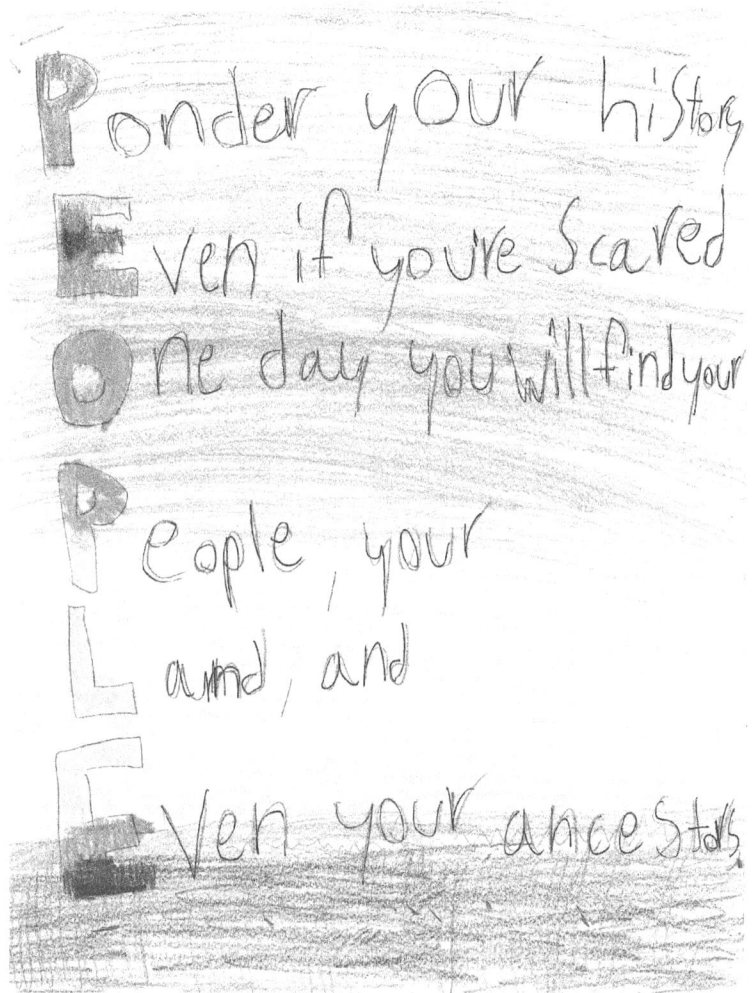

Student poem and artwork reflecting on our place-based unit exploring humanity through landscapes.

Does Place-Based Learning Really Fit with Organizing?

At this point, you might be thinking, "Well, place-based learning sounds great, but does it really fit with organizing?" It's a fair question! It's also a question rooted in the popular understanding of civic education today—not just civic education, but civic culture. That is, an understanding of civics that is divorced from geography and power. Union organizing is a window into how these two concepts are intrinsically linked.

In union organizing, the geography of the worksite was the source of power for laborers. Worksites for much of US labor history in the twentieth century drew workers to live in a specific geographic area. It was common for folks to work together, socialize together, worship together and raise their kids together. In this regard, work created deep social bonds and a culture of collective responsibility. Successful organizing meant understanding a specific place and people.

Worksite issues motivated union organizing, and still do to this day. Issues experienced on the shop floor (or classroom), like hazardous working conditions, brought workers together in conversation. Hearing the common experiences of one another, workers became united in their resolve to address those issues. If a worksite is unorganized, meaning it didn't have a union representing the collective voice of the laborers, these issues could form the basis of an organizing campaign.

Union organizing aided workers in the process of becoming certified, a process that changed over the course of the century in accordance with federal and state law. In essence, the process of starting a union amounts to a drive to have a majority of workers within the unit sign cards stating their support for the creation of a union, followed by an election run by the National Labor Relations Board (NLRB). If the election results in 50% plus one of the voting employees voting for a union, the NLRB will move to certify the union and the bargaining process for a first contract can start. Once an agreement is reached between the parties (labor and management), the contract needs to be ratified by the parties.

This being said, we must also acknowledge that the geography of work in the United States is deeply shaped and influenced by the legacy of racism. Segregation, reinforced by housing discrimination in the form of policies like red lining, restricted access to homes along racial lines. This historically unjust practice meant access to housing limited the proximity of work by race even after de jure segregation ended (Rothstein, 2017). In this regard, when we teach like an organizer, we must seek to have a critical understanding of place and labor history.

Our schools have their own history, shaped by housing, industry and working people. Coming into conversation with neighbors and coworkers about the past tells us more about the forces that shape our lives today—and it can get us and our students thinking about the forces beyond individuals that factor into the way we experience our daily lives. Both place-based learning and organizing share in common the ability to engage the individual in seeing themselves within a broader context. Both nudge us toward finding our own path to action in our context, and in so doing, tell us that we, together, can shape our civic space.

Challenge, Choice, Outcome Model

When I teach like an organizer, I know I need a story. It can be simple, but the narrative that we create for our schoolwork should be an invitation to the students to join in and enjoy the work that we're doing. The simple format that I frequently use is: challenge, choice, action (or outcome). This is borrowed from the former farmworker organizer turned Harvard Professor, Marshall Ganz (2016).

Ganz's model is the basis for what he calls "public narrative". The organizer who wants to create a public narrative must first go through the process of conducting many one-on-one conversations in the community that s/he seeks to work alongside. Each one-on-one is conducted with the intent of surfacing the interest, dreams and hope of each individual. The organizer can then look at the collection of interests within the community to determine the overarching story of the community. What issues are folks expressing as a primary concern? The organizer can then take that "research" and piece together a story that is compelling to her community. The intent being that the story will compel individuals within the community not just to share that common issue or hope, but to actually act on it by starting to be in conversation together.

In the classroom, we need to be listening to the stories, the dreams and hopes that students share. These can be the basis for our work together. Just like the community organizer listens for trends, suspending their own personal interests and judgment, a we too must practice this kind of intensely agnostic listening.

The longer that we teach a specific age or grade range, the more of a sense we gain of what to listen to and for. Not only that, but we start to anticipate the conversations that crop up at different parts of the year. The same advantage (maybe we can call it wisdom) comes from teaching in the same physical place year after year. We can start to feel the place. The key is that we have to stay feeling—stay connected to our own heart, head and gut. Otherwise, it can become easy to go numb with routine and allow the uniquely special occurrences of the place to start to blend into the background of daily life. Over time, teaching gives us that meta-data on what attracts student interest and what issues are recursive and intriguing for certain ages.

Educator and author David Sobel has picked up on some of these trends. Sobel (2008) proposes that we look at student engagement through the prism of the core design principles of: animal allies, mapping, adventure, special places, hunting and gathering, and small worlds. The concept of animal allies was touched upon in Chapter 1—viewing the world through the eyes of animals and seeking understanding of the animal world through empathy. Map making, which appears in this chapter, engages students in the geo-spatial relationships of their community. Hunting and gathering, which appears in Chapter 1, engages students in the physical search for found materials within the community space. Small worlds, which are discussed in this chapter, involve exploring scale and miniaturizing the social and natural landscapes to allow for higher levels of hands-on design and creation. Finally, adventure provides students with a narrative element that drives exploration and enthusiasm for the subject. In my experience, Sobel's study of student interests, expressed in these core design principles, meshes well with the idea of "public narrative".

The River of DOOM: Challenge, Choice, Outcome

As the rain lifted and dense fog hugged the ground, the class walked to the edge of the stream. Brenda's eyes moved quickly from one embankment to the other in search of another frog. The quest for the aquatic animals of the

Cooperative Middle School (the name of our middle school) was on! Could we find and map the locations of these secretive critters? The choice was simple: create a map, gather data on sightings or sketch out a scene as we moved upstream. One boy would later share his sketch with me. It was titled, "The River of Doom".

Alongside our school there is a drainage culvert. The culvert easily stretches over the distance of 300 yards, but the scraggly trees that line the edges of the culvert make it difficult to see its end. Our class of sixth graders loved the culvert, which they call "the river". It's where we found a frog with

River of Doom.

five legs in the Fall of 2023. As one can imagine, the culvert is a place of excitement and mystery. The culvert is also the kind of place that would be completely ignored on most school grounds and really wouldn't be a factor in most classes.

I used the challenge, choice, outcome framework to guide our simple expedition. Here's a short example of a student-facing prompt using the framework:

Challenge: Travel up the "River of Doom" and document your findings. Look for animals, landmarks and potential pitfalls!
Choice: Pick a job within your group. Be a wildlife tracker, a travel journalist or a cartographer and decide what kind of visuals will help you tell the story of the journey up the "River of Doom."
Outcome: Create a drawing, short story or map that tells a story about what you found in the area that can be shared with your peers.

Note: Putting students in the physical environment creates an opportunity for students to express their observations on the world as it is. It is also a chance for conversations about the world as it should be.

Agitation: Activating the Imagination Using Stories

I arrive early to school and post a sign on my classroom door at one point in the Fall. The sign reads something like, "This room has been closed per the order of the Stratham Police Department." Then, I pull the shade on the door down, close all the blinds, shut off the lights and lock the door.

Students are puzzled when they arrive at school for homeroom—their "spidey senses" are just tingling. They all have this gut feeling that something is afoot—and they're right. I tell them all sorts of different things as I take homeroom attendance in the hallway. I say that I've been asked by the police to not let anyone into the room. "But why?" they want to know. "I'm sorry, it's official police business", I say, before pausing to add, "I've been asked not to comment". They wiggle the handle to the locked door and want to know, "Where will class be if we can't have it in there?" I muster enough voice to give a gravely halfhearted, "I just don't know", as I look around doubtfully, searching for answers to the question of whether there will even be class...ever again.

The first bell rings. Students are released from their various homerooms and head toward their first classes of the morning. There is more confusion, more hesitation about my class. I call them to make a semicircle sitting on the floor in front of me in the hall.

"As some of you have noticed", I start, "the door to the classroom is closed". "The fact is the Stratham Police have asked me to not let anyone into the classroom. And I can't comment, so please don't ask me to". I can feel the tension. "Some of you may have smelled the bad smell that has been seeping out of the room", I continue. At this point, everyone starts to sniffle and those closest to the classroom try to peer through the crack between the bottom of the door and floor—looking for the airflow that may be carrying the stink.

Cutting them off midsniff, I say, "Well, if it's okay with you all, I would like to tell you a little bit about my strange morning. It started like all my mornings, with a nice walk of my dogs. As you know, my dogs Louie and Lola are always getting into trouble. And this morning was no different".

This often elicits a few, "Oh, my dog is always getting into trouble" and "You'll never guess what my dog rolled in last weekend, Mr. Goodwin". I press on.

"We headed out to the trail behind my house. As you might remember, my house is very old. And we're constantly finding different things in the woods. We found an old Coca-Cola bottle...and all sorts of stuff. I don't know what got into me this morning, but I decided to let Lola off the leash. She went running ahead on the trail and for a while I didn't see her. Then I heard a yelp. With Louie's leash in my hands, I went searching. I heard her scratching something. She was digging and digging and digging. I took her by the collar and gently as I could, I pulled her back. With my other hand, I reached down in the pre-dawn light and my hand hit it. I could feel it. It was smooth and as I lifted it up, I could see it was white. That's when I took out my phone and called the police. They told me to bring in what I had found as completely as possible—so I did."

At this point, the kids are leaning forward listening to the story. Even the ones who are doubting my story have a look on their face that tells me that they want it to be true. That one look that tells me that we're heading in the right direction as a class—not just for this day and lesson—but it's a sign that students want to play, that they want to help create a world of imagination. Imaginative play is special, and it takes us as a class agreeing to suspend the "rules of school" for the period of play. And in that time, we can inhabit a different time and place. It's an agreement that young children make so easily, readily and frequently between one another, and I find that students in late childhood and early adolescents are still so intrigued by it, but need a bit more of a formal invitation to participate. Stories are that kind of invitation.

This is where I introduce the social proof for my story, the school resource officer or the student aid in the classroom. Usually, I ask for their help with the story the day before. If it's the resource officer, I'll say to the students, "Hey, there's the officer now ... Officer Smith, I know you said that we couldn't go in the room, but is there any way that I can show the kids what I found?" The officer will look at me, shake her head and look at the kids. "Okay, Mr. Goodwin, but just this once". And with that I walk to the classroom door and ask the students to not rush in and to slowly follow me into the dark.

Eerie music is already playing from my speaker as they enter the room. Slowly, we walk to a long table in the darkest part of the room. Everyone gathers around the table. "I'm going to show you what I found", I state in a serious voice. "Are you sure you want to see?" I ask. "Yes!" many shout. I slowly start to lift up a corner of the blanket, but then put it down quickly. "No, no, I can't...", I say. They grow mad and shout, "Show us!" "Okay, okay", and I swiftly pull back the blanket, letting go a gasp of horror as I do. Some students close their eyes, some shout and others back away, anticipating disgust. Others gleefully look on as the contours of a skeleton are revealed.

Just like in a fun house, or in a movie, there are students who want to break the imaginative spell shouting, "it's fake!" Yet, those who like to be the first to assert the claim are revealing how much fun they've been having following the story. So, I try to keep them in it for just a little longer. "Wait, look closely", I say to reel them back in and have them take a second look. "What's that...?"

One student, who is close, sees it too. "It's a piece of paper", he cries! "Quick, open it up", I enthuse. The class huddles around the note. It's hard to read. I wrote it while staging the room with a very shaking hand. "Under the desk?" one student suggests to the others. "Yes, yes, it says under the desk". And with that we all go to our hands and knees looking under the desks in search of another clue.

They find a small piece of paper taped to the bottom of a chair after searching under the table-chair combo desks that are scattered around the room. Again, struggling to make out the squiggly handwriting in the dim light, a couple students make out that it says "Green, read me page 577". "It must be a book!"

"Grab books!" I shout, as I finish passing out the paper for our next step. Students flip through the green books in the room and find the page where there is a world map.

"Nice work, so far", I say, "But the hunt is just starting...".

Imaginative Play

Imaginative play suspends the rules of reality for a moment on the condition of trust. If I trust you, I believe that we can have fun together. Play isn't just something that we do when we have some free time. Play is essential to what makes us human. It is the core of social life and how we relate to one another. From our very early days, researchers have found that we laugh as a form of social interaction. We laugh before we speak. That should tell us something about the importance of laughter and play to our social development.

Knowing our students require this kind of social space, we create a playful learning environment. The environment needs to invite students to join in on the fun that is our learning. That's why I'll turn the front of my room into a stage for acting or transform the room into a court of justice, the inner depths of a pyramid or even a food truck festival (more on all these later). It's also why I'll have stations where students can paper-mache, cut and build. All of these activities are things that we can do together, ways that we can transform the class together—and all actions that require us to use our imagination.

Play is abandoned around the time of middle school. Instead, students go into sports programs and more structured extra-curricular activities. Many schools give up on time for free play in the day as if when you turn ten or eleven years old you stop needing recess. It is still needed. We continue to benefit from learning to navigate social situations that arise from peer-to-peer play. While more recess and outdoor time is critical, my argument here is that we can use class time as a means of adding social learning to our day with play.

Start small by using a creative hook for a lesson or unit. Get students engaged with the ideas and show them that it's okay to be a little silly. Along the way, test your "teacher's gut" and see how students are responding. We can always make adjustments. When students know that you are willing to be part of the learning too, they feel that much more comfortable taking the "risk" of having fun in school.

The civic imagination can only flourish when we can access our imagination. Play is the primary method of accessing the imagination for students all the way into late childhood and early adolescents.

Imaginative play is the gateway for the civic imagination. If we can play together, we can dream together. These experiences are the root of our shared social world. They are how we get to know one another and be known. The dreams that we have together as children and adolescents are the basis for us imagining the "world as it should be" and these seeds of possibility are dependent on a vibrant and playful life.

Self, Us, Now

The saying, "People before program", means that we must come to know our people through the stories that they tell. To do so, we focus our energies on unlocking stories together through co-creation. This is possible through the use of a framework like "challenge-choice-outcome". Playing with and constructing narratives can turn run of the mill assignments into voyages to the depth of the earth, treks into the unknown reaches of dark forests and ramblings into ancient history.

Another layer of the public narrative framework that we can use in class is: "self-us-now". While the "challenge, choice, outcome" structure drives narratives forward because of its sequential nature, "self-us-now" provides for more fluidity. For example, if you want to start with the "story of now" that works. If you prefer to start with the "story of self" that works too. Folks who are very comfortable with the framework sometimes weave in and out of the various three aspects. Each element of the narrative structure turns into a guidepost for expression rather than concrete structures of permanence and rigidity.

Many who are just starting to use this framework like to start off with the "story of now". The "problem of now" is the issue that "your people" feel most acutely at the moment. In this case, "your people" are the people who we want to bring together—our class. In organizing work, the "problem of now" is surfaced by the organizer through extensive one-on-one conversations. After those conversations, the organizer analyzes their conversations for the "greatest common denominator"—that is the issue that can be articulated in a compelling way that affects the most people or affects people the most deeply. The organizer then considers their own personal experiences, asking herself, "how do I relate to the problem of now?" This leads the organizer to create "The story of self", a short explanation relating the speaker to the "problem of now". Finally, the "story of us" shows the affected group that the problem that I am facing now is the problem that you are facing and that other people are facing—which is why we need to act together now to solve the problem.

Ganz (2016) connects each part of the public narrative framework to the questions of Rabbi Hillel. Hillel asked: "If I am not for myself, who will be for me?" "If I am for myself alone, what am I?" "If not now, when?" The story of self is our answer to the first question. This is especially important for those of us who are uncomfortable talking about ourselves, because if we cannot explain why an issue is important to us and how we relate to it—we will be shutting ourselves off from relating to other people, our students included. In this way, we are called to tell our story of self, not out of vanity but out of a sense of generosity. Sharing our story is an act of vulnerability that opens us to the world. While we open ourselves to hurt by sharing it, we also open ourselves to others who are vulnerable and others who have experienced what we have experienced. In that act, we are stepping into public life. We are forging new relationships that previously were not there.

Within the public narrative framework, we build upon our personal story by seeking to unite our people around a shared common experience. That is why, as Hillel's second question suggests, "we cannot just tell our own story. We cannot just be for ourselves alone". This brings us to present the story of "us"—to explore who "we" are and how "we" are all affected by the problem of now.

Hillel's final question brings us to the moment we are facing. It's a focusing question and a question of urgency. "If not now, when?" It brings to mind how we can plan for action and act together. This final question is a chance to guide "our people" toward the first "next step"—and invite them into initiating and participating in a plan of action.

To use this public narrative structure without providing actionable steps is to create frustration and reinforce passivity and apathy. The absence of actionable steps implicitly tells our people, "Yes, I have experienced the issue, and we share the issue, but really there is nothing that we can do about it". In this manner, using the public narrative framework creates the invitation to participate in solving the issues that we have in common. This is the kind of working together that creates community through a form of engagement that seeks to use all the talents of the community. Widespread contribution is the source of belonging, an antidote to the isolation that so many feel today.

Teaching Tip: Using Public Narrative As a Hook

Try to use the "self, us, now" framework as a way to create a story for a unit hook. The hook will then connect students to an ongoing issue in the world, compelling them to take action by getting engaged with the issue and learning more! Starting with the "problem of now" can be a good way to approach writing this kind of hook for students as it will allow you to be intentional about specific curricular content that you will want to relate in your public narrative as a hook.

The Advocacy v. Organizing Mindset in Civics

How Can the Organizing Perspective Shift Our Civic Gaze (and Practice)?

The use of the organizing model as the basis for civic education presents a consequential shift in perspective in civic learning. The progressive educational philosopher,

Boyd Bode (1937), wrote about the need to reconsider what constitutes education for democracy. Writing nearly 100 years ago, he identified the desire that many of us teachers feel to this day that civics too often is dry. Our parched lips, cracking from speaking the word, "change" are tormented further in this time of thirst for civic knowledge. Yet, Bode says, without a new source of water, we, the educators, are left to wander in the desert with our divining rods or return to the old well that is traditionalism. The organizing model presents one such alternative to these rather bleak choices.

One aspect of traditionalism in civics is the perspective of the single person developing the solutions on his/her own. This perspective has been institutionalized in the form of the aforementioned bureaucrat, who although meaning well, did not invite the people affected by the issue to participate in solving it. This approach leaves the people affected by the issue on the sidelines and perpetuates a culture of dependency on the expert. The expert reinforces his/her position as a distiller of wisdom, a fount of solutions. After all, it's easier for him/her to figure things out on his/her own than to broaden support and build a bigger tent. Luckily, teaching like an organizer is all about building a bigger tent!

To start, broadening the tent means learning from the inclinations of the bureaucratic and individualistic mindset. In districts where students take on civic action projects where they are identifying issues—oftentimes, the issues that students chose are ones that are based on their experience. This can be great in the sense that students are learning about issues that are important and relevant to their lives. In my mind, any civic work is good work. It's all a step onto the ladder of engagement. At the same time, we, as teachers, can also keep in mind that this kind of issue selection process can lead to more advocacy than organizing. The individual has their own issue and they are going to research that issue and talk about that issue, maybe they'll present to other groups about that issue. This is all very one-directional work. In this way, the student becomes the expert and then becomes the distiller of knowledge. This can be an experience that feels empowering to the student. It yields sharpened advocates for a divided world—and to an extent that is the world that we live in.

The organizing model doesn't empower—it seeks to bring together power that already exists. Unlike models of civic education that stress individualism, the organizing model is based on the idea that what we need is inherent, present and often latent. What we seek exists in each of us and it takes all of us working together to be able to actualize the civic dreams that we hold.

The organizing model emphasizes the communal nature of change over time. When we know that change starts with listening to all the issues that are in the room, we open ourselves to integrating our lived experiences with those of the people next to us. We do this not because our personal experiences don't matter or that they should be subsumed by the group. No, instead we listen in this manner to find ourselves. We find ourselves in others. And in finding ourselves in others (and allowing others to find us) we find our true selves. This is the very root of social learning; it's peer referential and self-affirming.

The affirming nature of this kind of communal learning provides implicit lessons about change too. We are teaching that when we slow the civic change process down to the level of the individual and engage in deep listening that there is room for consensus building and there is room for people who would not otherwise be in alignment. These observable facts also teach that change isn't about imposing the researched position from above on the group, but that change and solutions are generated together.

Now, I would like to emphasize that I am suggesting that organizing creates room for consensus and the possibility of bringing together disparate views. This is not to say the consensus is always necessary. I am simply saying there is a possibility. When we listen to one another without a predetermined solution waiting in our pocket, there is simply a greater chance that we will hear from our partner, understand their issues and start to nurture seeds of solutions that we can further develop together. The development is dependent upon us further nurturing our relationship, bringing in new partners and taking action. None of this is given.

Speed is the strength of the advocacy model of civics. It's quick in that we can "go it alone" and that it can teach us the power of research, messaging and knowing your audience. It promises that if we can get the message right, we can "win people to our side". It also teaches us that if we don't "win people to our side" or if we "build it and they don't come" then there must have been a problem with the message or the messenger. These are all relevant lessons to the current discourse on civics—yet, they are not all the lessons that are relevant.

The organizing model presents both flexibility to practitioners and holds the potential to impart more durable and sustainable lessons. It meets the needs of students and teachers on the ground by practicing coalition building methods. The organizing model doesn't seek to replace advocacy, after all advocacy can be a helpful tool. Rather, the organizing model is instructive as to a more healthy practice of civics through building a more well-rounded set of skills and dispositions that can be used by our students over the course of their lives in the public sphere. In so doing, teaching like an organizer may be just the thing to end this arid season of civic drought.

Reading Public Narrative and Digging Deeper

We will next look into how students and teachers as organizers can learn to read emerging public narratives. As we hold one-on-one conversations, we gain a sense for the issues that people are facing. I've previously mentioned how the organizer may step back after conducting a sample set of one-on-ones and analyze those conversations (their data) to determine the unifying issue. This being the topic that has the potential of being deeply and widely felt. This is the work of the "head". We are thinking logically and analytically, sorting, labeling and rationalizing. Adding to this mix, we also need to remember to be thinking with our heart. In each one-on-one, we need to get a sense of the emotional feeling of the moment. How are people feeling about the issue? Recording these thoughts and feelings after each meeting can help you keep track of how things are trending. These notes will help you to read the emerging public narrative and can help you shape the narrative to speak to the patterns of the heart that you are deciphering.

Reading Emotions and Co-Constructing the Public Narrative

Inertia-Urgency
Apathy-Anger
Isolation-Belonging
Fear-hope
Self-doubt—You can make a difference

*Ganz (2016)

Our knowledge of emotional tensions (diagrammed above) helps us to read the patterns of the heart that emerge from the conversations we have with our people, our students. We live with many of these tensions every day. Just like we discussed in Chapter 1, the organizer must operate in the "world as it is" while keeping an eye set on the vision of the "world as it should be". The organizer creates tension by operating between these two points, tension that can be resolved through action. In this case, our understanding of emotional tension allows us to create a narrative that motivates our people to move to action. The feeling of inertia is overcome by urgency. Apathy is overcome by anger. Isolation is overcome by belonging, fear is overcome with hope and self-doubt is overcome by making a difference.

Looking at the table of emotional tension (above), ask yourself if you have seen these emotions in your classroom.

As teachers, we are constantly trying to move students to action using deadlines. That is creating a sense of urgency to move what feels like inertia.

As teachers, we teach hard histories and tough truths, raising the righteous sense of anger among students who ask, "how could the world be like this?" This is anger moving beyond apathy.

As teachers, especially after the pandemic, we tried to help students to see themselves in school and to feel a deep sense of belonging in school. This was a direct effect of the need to both overcome the isolation that we felt from being out of school and also the social isolation that so many of us feel today because of the antisocial medium of social media.

As teachers, we try to inspire hope for a better future among our students, we use connection and experience to dispel fear, building trust and relationships.

And as teachers, we accompany our students on the journey of making a difference, showing each the power they can have in the classroom and community—proving that self-doubt was misplaced. It's so important to see that we are already so aware of these emotional tensions. They guide so much of our work from the day to day to the big picture of why we do what we do.

Our consciousness of emotional tension can increase the effectiveness of our organizing capacities in the classroom. We can weave the emotional tensions that are facing our community into the framework of "self-us-now" to create a public narrative that engages our students and calls them to act. What's more, by modeling the use of the public narrative, even in a simple form, we can help students to learn how to use the framework themselves.

Learning to read emotion within our public stories helps us to understand those with whom we share our community. Undoubtedly, students will hear stories of isolation, fear and apathy. Providing them with the background knowledge of how to overcome challenges and create positive narratives of perseverance, hope and making a difference moves us toward having agency within our community. If we can read public narrative and understand how it operates within our community, we can write our own narratives that inspire positive growth and relationality in our own little corner of the world. I'm reminded of the wonderful zines produced by Ricardo Morales (2025)—where he suggests that narratives are what make our communal soil rich and fertile. Without narratives, we cannot sustain our beliefs or bring about change we would like to see in the world. Morales asks, "what narrative would make your soil healthier?" It is my hope that the introduction and construction of narratives as a tool for teaching like an organizer elevate their important civic power—cultivating healthier soil in every community.

Map Relationships

Early in this chapter, I introduced the idea of mapping as a means of getting to know our community and the area surrounding our school. This section will extend the use of mapping to relationships. Relationship mapping is a foundational concept in organizing as it shows how people are interacting with issues in their lives and in the community. Relationship mapping is a way that we can try to see connections that otherwise may be invisible to us. Visualizing relationships and connections allows us to analyze communications between different parts of the learning community (or community at large) and then act to improve the relationships.

Maps convey key information succinctly, making them a key tool in the field of organizing. In union organizing, "power mapping" is a phrase that is used to describe the social connections between workers. It can also be referred to as "relational mapping". Relational mapping asks us to think about the relational ties between folks at the workplace. Who knows who? Who has kids in the same grade? Who went to college together?, etc. All of these questions are relevant to the organizer because relationship is the building block of power. When we know where the relationships are and when we know the depth of the relationships, there is a better chance of understanding the people who make up our community. With this understanding, we can bring people together to help them to work on the issues that are important to their lives.

The map that you create for tracking relationships at your school doesn't need to be fancy. It just needs to be functional. It can be useful for students who are getting to know their teachers. The relational map that you create might start with the people that you know best—likely the classrooms that are closest to yours. Your students can sketch the hall and the rough physical layout of the classes. Having a note section to write down what you know and find out about different people and their interests can help you develop a baseline record that may be helpful when you expand your map. Here's a basic example:

My Mr. Goodwin Notes: Has worked here 11 yrs	Hall	Ms. Glynn Notes: Advises debate club, taught here 2 years
Mr. Belanger Notes: coaches softball		Mrs. Delgado Notes: Like genealogy, Friends with Mr. Belanger, started teaching in 1995

Classroom map.

Another way that can be helpful to map relationships is the bubble map. The bubble map shows the central place that we are studying and the social connections between each of the people involved. For example, the central place could be the classroom (shown in the diagram below). We write "our class" in the center of what will be our bubble map and draw a circle around the two words. Next, we can consider the physical groupings in the classroom.

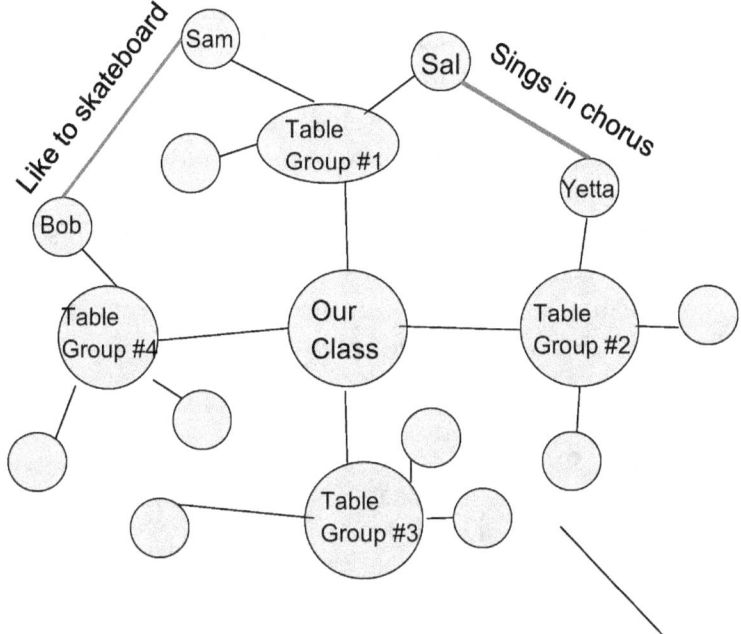

Bubble map.

In my class, we usually have four or five small groups of desks. So we can draw four lines coming out of the "our class bubble" and add the words, "table group #1" at the end of the first line and draw a circle around the words. We repeat this step for each of the table groups. Next, for each table group we can add little offshoot bubbles with the names of the different students who sit at those table groups. Now, the fun part! With a different color (I chose purple) draw a line of connection between the people in the class with shared interests. Sam and Bob both like skateboarding, so I draw my purple connection line between their names and write about their shared interest. We can do this as a class activity early on to look for commonalities. We might ask, "Can you find a connection you share with each person in the class?"

We can adapt the bubble map once this has been introduced, if your class is comfortable with the general format. For example, if your students are working on a civic action project, you can use the map to help students understand the issues that they are interested in and how those interests are connected. We might generate a list of possible issues after conducting one-on-ones in the class. From this list we select what appear to be the most popular choices. Students can write these issues into their diagrams.

Ask students to group themselves at table groups according to who shares those interests. As each student moves to the group that interests them, they can add themselves to the diagram and each person in the class can add them to the diagram. This leads to Sal and Sam adding themselves to the group interested in the issue of creating a skate park. It also leads Bob and Hannah adding their names to the issue of library hours.

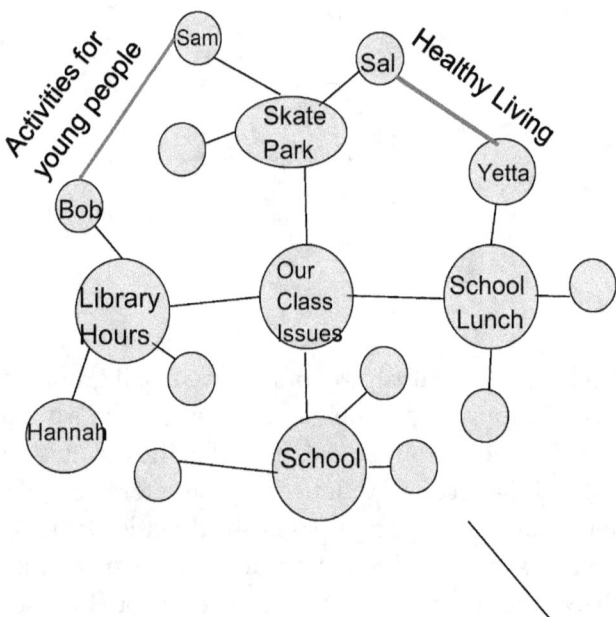

Community issues bubble map.

Next, the groups can look for what might connect the different issues groups based on one-on-one conversations. Students can indicate who they talked to on the chart by drawing a line between themselves and their conversation partner. For example, Sal and Yetta found that the issues of creating a skate park and the issue of improving school lunches might share the common thread of healthy living. Connecting people and issues provides for potential collaboration between issue groups, a seed of coalition building. As a baseline, this activity gets different issue groups talking to one another about their goals and commonalities. Seeking this kind of common ground is important, especially as groups may start to specialize in different issues.

Snowflakes

Learning to visualize relationships helps our students to see and track social interactions concretely. For this reason, another popular way to describe mapping social connection is the visual of the snowflake. The snowflake is a shape that is unique—no two are alike. The pattern of each snowflake also repeats within itself, it's a fractal. This means that the snowflake can be a perfect model to visualize the unique and repeating social patterns within our own communities.

The practical application of the snowflake as a model for mapping social change and connection starts with place. In our case, the place is the classroom. If we have five students who are interested in extending the library hours in town as their issue—then each of those five students needs to go out and have one-on-one conversations with people in the community about extending library hours. Their one-on-ones need to end with an "ask" seeking more commitment from the person and determining if the person knows three to five other people who would also like to see the hours of the library extended. In this manner, the students are starting as the central "hub" of the snowflake and building out a "hub" of another five people—and the pattern repeats. Information can flow back and forth between different snowflakes, hearing each other's needs and responding to one another in kind. This network is maintained on the principle of reciprocity and shared commitment to the values of the community. In the case of learning communities, such as in the classroom, this tangible image can help us to practice creating networks of communication that are organic to the student experience, rather than mediated through technology. The fractal change model presents a way to visualize our connections through our expanding networks.

Try it out: The Conversation Web (Adapted from *Inquiry Illuminated*, Mitchell, 2019)

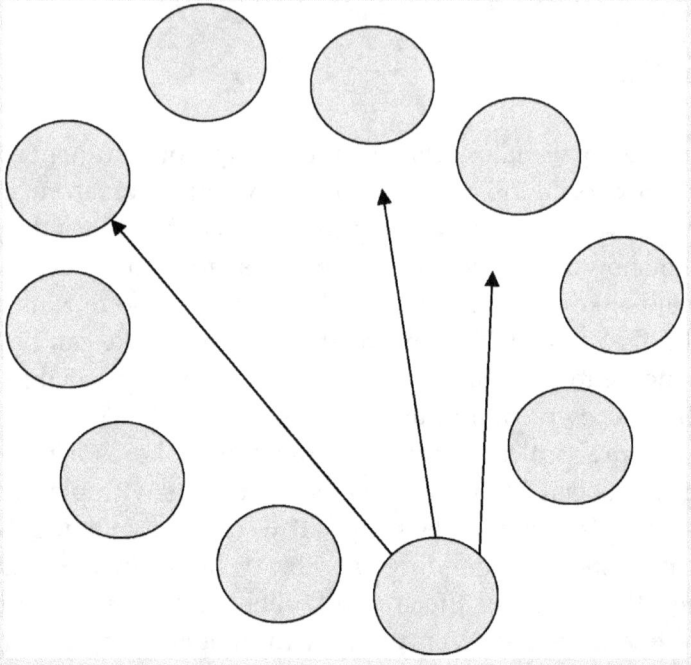

Conversation Web

During classroom discussions, it can be tricky to track all the different contributions that students make. It can also be tricky for students to track the flow of conversations or know what to do when other people are speaking.

One tool to use is the conversation web. Create diagrams of your seating chart that you can use during a class discussion (or start the class by giving each student a blank piece of paper where they can sketch the seating arrangement.

To start, ask each student to track the speaking of one other student. I usually say something like, "make eye contact with that one person that you will be observing". Then I'll do a quick scan of the room to see if anyone doesn't have a partner to observe during the conversation. (continued below)

Here are three different approaches that you can use for tracking the conversation. Sometimes it's best to start at "Level 1" and have the students show what they can do before having them move to Level 2 or 3 the next time you have a discussion.

Level 1—Ask students to draw an arrow whenever the person they are observing directs a comment or question at another person. It's simple. It might look like the diagram above.

Level 2—Ask students to draw a line of connection between the person who speaks and the person or people who respond to what is said. Speaking includes questions and comments. This creates a big (and messy) web. It gives us a sense of the flow of the conversation, who was involved, and who was not involved.

Level 3—Give students two colored pencils. Create a small key in the bottom right of your seating diagram. In the key, pick one color to represent questions and one to represent statements. When the person you are observing asks a question to a specific person, use your "question pencil" to draw a line. If the person you are observing asks a question generally to the class (or unspecified person), draw a line to the person who responds with your "question pencil". If the question is not responded to, draw a line with your "question pencil" to the bottom of your page where you can have "parking lot". Write the unanswered question in the parking lot. Use your "comment pencil" to draw lines from the person you are observing to anyone with whom that person directs or exchanges comments.

Reflection Questions: What does your web show/tell us? Who did you speak to? Were there peers who were not involved in the conversation? What could we (or you personally) do to involve more people in the discussion?

What Relationship Mapping in NOT

Mapping can be a form of data entry. We write down and keep track of who we meet, gathering contact information that can be used now or later. Database development is a tool that both non-organizers and organizers employ. For organizers, these data are a point of contact to be used for personal relationship development over the long term. For marketers, database development and mapping is more transactional. It's about sending promotional deals and pop-up advertisements—microtargeting, monitoring and selling. The mapping, organizing and relationship building that we're aiming for is distinctly in the organizing camp—our work is to build the kind of social relationships that make our communities civic spaces of generative growth and empowerment.

Are We a Welcoming Community?

I was asked to teach a unit on immigration one year. After reading novels about the topic of immigration in the United States, we created a human timeline. Each student picked an event, which related to laws and major events in US immigration history. The event descriptions were relatively short and each fit on a small slip of paper. After reading their event, students summarized the event in their own words and explained why they thought this event might matter today. We sorted ourselves around the classroom from the earliest event to the most recent and shared what we found.

The juxtaposition of the laws and events lends itself to the organizing framework: the world as it is and the world as it should be. That, in many ways, is the history of American immigration: the harsh reality of a new land that is often exclusionary and the idealism of a country of newcomers. One law that leapt off the page to students was the Chinese Exclusion Act of 1882, which banned immigration of workers from China for ten years. I also include the famous Emma Lazarus poem *The New Colossus*, which was published in 1883. Lazarus's poem was later added as a plaque to the Statue of Liberty in 1903. Students don't miss the opportunity to point out the contrast between barring an entire peoples' entry into the country in one year and the celebration of America as a beacon of hope and a "mother of exiles" in the next. Students want to know, how can these two things exist in the same place? This is the kind of question that lingers in the air of a classroom.

Middle schoolers are gripped by questions of inclusion. Many have the visceral sense of the changing social dynamics that lead long-time friends to join new groups at lunch. In the following days, in my attempt to move our discussion toward the immediate, I remind the students of the human immigration timeline that we constructed. Then, I shift to rely on the words of a student, posing the question that a student had asked me on the way out of the room: "Are we welcoming as a school?" It was a question that cut to the point: We have an obligation to live our values. We can act. Yes, history is filled with contradictions, but what about us, here, now? All of these thoughts drove and animated our discussion that day and in following classes.

"What would it look like if we were welcoming?" I asked the classes.

"Well, it might depend on who we were welcoming", one girl pointed out. "I don't like to presume I know how other people might or might not like to be welcomed".

"Okay", I responded, "how would you like to be received and welcomed at the school? One third of our school is new each year—we welcome an entire grade of 6th graders and new students who join us from other schools too."

Working together, teams of students developed lists of what they would like to see at our school as signs of welcoming. The indicators included: pride flags and stickers, posters showing students of diverse backgrounds, classrooms labeled in braille and labels in languages other than English, sports and equipment for students who have accessibility needs, student artwork, single stall bathrooms and student-led tours for students who join the school midway in the year.

We made a class list of "welcoming indicators" so students could see the various ideas posted in the room. Groups of students were invited to borrow ideas from one another too. Once we had discussed the class's ideas for indicators, we created t-charts. On the left-hand side of the t-chart, students wrote down the indicators that they were most interested in tracking. We left space for our observations on the right-hand side of the t-chart. Our school had developed a fire-safety map that provided a visual layout of the school, which I offered to each of the groups. The map was used to highlight where students found their indicators. Finding an indicator could also mean having a conversation with a student or an adult in the school about their indicators.

With that, we slowly walked the hallways of the school looking to identify any indicators that we could find. We benefited from many gracious conversations on the part of my colleagues along the way. Of course, students wanted to look into each classroom—and sometimes they did. I encouraged them to not interrupt classes and to keep closed doors closed. Students noted their findings on their t-chart trackers and highlighted the map of the school as they encountered new indicators.

We got together back in the classroom to discuss the initial findings once we had walked through the entire school. I placed three large sheets of paper around our room, each with a different prompt: What stood out to you? What was missing? What should we do about it? This question set focused our data interpretation on present conditions (and possible positives), areas that could be potential growth zones for the future based on the current conditions, and then the action we could take to possibly narrow that gap between the present and the future.

I passed out sticky notes for the students to write their responses down on, encouraging students to reflect on their own findings. One boy wrote, "I've walked these halls each day and I never noticed what I saw until just now". This sticky note stood out as an example of how we can build our critical awareness of the world around us. Our minds swiftly blend so much of our experience in familiar places into the background. Some say that blending the familiar into the background helps us to manage our overall cognitive load. It takes practice to train our mind to intentionally slow down and analyze the familiar. When we do, we can gain new insights and improve the issues affecting our daily lives.

Starting with contradictions creates intellectual space for questions in a classroom. Contradictions invite students to puzzle over how to reach a point of resolution. While we can discuss historical and hypothetical resolutions—these discussions often open the door to critical self-analysis. We would be hypocrites if we analyzed and offered recommendations for improving the lives of others without considering our own responsibilities. Asking questions about school refocuses our daily experience as the site of inquiry. Mapping visually displays the social terrain where we can find answers to our questions. The truths that we encounter through mapping the immediate reminds students that they too have a say in how we become a more welcoming place, both now and into the future.

Conclusion on Relationship Mapping

Mapping relationships helps us to visualize the social terrain that we so often walk. Ironically, our familiarity with the social terrain of our lives often obscures it to us and hides what otherwise might be helpful clues about the web of activity that connects us to community. Taking the time to map our conversations, we can start to see how physical space is shaped and shapes social interaction. We can start to see the barriers that may be interrupting or disrupting access to greater social cohesion. When we make our thinking visible, we have a better chance of taking our individual thoughts and ideas about the way the world works and open those thoughts and ideas to group analysis. In the process, ideas are tested and refined, yielding actionable information to the community of learners.

Issues v. Problems: What Is the Difference?

One source of frustration for organizers and changemakers is mistaking a problem for an issue. While at face value, it's easy to think that these two similar words are interchangeable. They are not. Problems are big. They may be systemic (think of climate change). Problems are ultra-alluring. They tend to attract a lot of advocacy work—and dollars. But problems are just that—a problem.

Problems inspire a hazy commitment. They inspire a general feeling that something is wrong without a path to action. Yes, something is wrong, but there is a feeling that not much can be done about it. This can be a difficult thing to sort out for the organizer. The feeling that not much can be done about a situation is often due to years of nothing being done. Other times, the haziness of problems provides comfort by knowing about the problem, and in knowing about it, understanding that it's just so big that individual action won't solve it—excusing individuals from engaging.

The lack of a path to action means that the problems can't really be owned by the community. Instead, the problem remains the possession of the expert or "leader". This reinforces the concept of the established leader doing the work, which in turn, diminishes the overall power and efficacy of the community as a magnifier of change. The theory of action of the organizer must be always focused on supporting the community in coming together to address the issues that affect their lives. Getting stuck in the "problem zone" prevents the community from taking meaningful action.

When it feels like the conversation is leading us toward a problem, turn to a different conversation—one about issues. Explore the topic from the perspective of the person who you are in conversation with. Clarifying questions that we can ask to gain a better understanding of the person and the issues they may be facing are: How are you affected? What is one thing you would do? Do others feel this way? Who or what is causing this? Keep your questions short. Let the person explain their thinking. Respecting the person's understanding and experience helps us to later integrate what they share with us into community action in the future. And in the end, trust your gut to tell you how the person might join with others to address the issue.

Sorting Problems and Issues with Students

Photo from the Philadelphia Metro.

Which are problems and which are issues? Write these words and phrases on index cards. Create one pack of cards per group in your class. Ask students to sort the cards into two categories: problems and issues. Provide students with simple definitions. Problems are big and can be systemic. Issues are small and action can be taken to resolve them in the near term. Ask students to be ready to justify their choices.

> Dog poop on the street
> Ending standardized testing
> Longer recess
> Better school lunches
> End climate change
> More school dances
> A recycling program for the school
> Better school clubs
> A no homework policy
> Stop selling plastic bags in town
> Ending sweatshops
> Banning straws
> End war
> Create a fair immigration system
> End hunger
> End homelessness
> I get more money on my birthday than some people earn all year
> More afterschool programs

Reflection: Pair groups together. Invite one group to present to the other group. Then have the groups switch. What were the areas where the two groups agreed? Any disagreements? What was the rationale of each group on the words when there was disagreement? How can recognizing the difference between issues and problems help?

Extension: Based on one-on-one conversations with your students (or a brainstorm) have your students create their own list of issues and problems for the activity.

In the end, we want to stimulate thinking in our class about what is possible when we work together. Starting to be able to distinguish between our problems and issues allows for us to make change pocket sized. That pocket-sized change gives us the chance to build a collective sense of agency that starts on small-scale issues and builds up. An issue isn't unimportant just because it is small. In fact, issues that seem small (and maybe trivial) are a powerful tool of noticing and relationship building. Slowly, we grow our imagination and learn how to act together. At the same time, we are always affirming the relationships in the classroom, looking to uplift the good that we see. These efforts take time and patience on the part of the teacher-as-organizer, including patience with oneself as we stretch and grow.

Conclusion

We can start to see the generative possibilities in the class when we follow the maxim, "People before program". We give ourselves permission to be intentional about creating a classroom space that invites in the stories of our students. The snippets of stories and the glimpses of interests that we gain from the start of the year are seeds of relationships that can grow over the course of a year—and a lifetime.

When we approach teaching as an organizer, we start to think expansively about the classroom experience. Place-based learning complements this expansive view of the classroom and community as a site of learning. We can shrink the community down to the miniature size, applying Sobel's (2008) principles—creating miniature cities, like Mossington, DC. We also use imagination to suspend reality and invite students to pursue adventures in schools, like traveling back in time. And we can use stories and maps to understand and express the relationships, emotions and complex dynamics of change that undergird our daily lives.

As teachers, we think of the long-term development of our students through the year experience—and yet, we also recognize that some lessons sink in years, or decades later.

Creating Mossington, DC.

Works Cited

Bode, B. (1937). *Democracy as a way of life*. MacMillan Co.
Chambers, E. T., & Cowan, M. A. (2003). *Roots for radicals*. Continuum.
Dopirak, K., & Neal, C. S. (2020). *Hurry up!: A book about slowing down*. Beach Lane Books.
Emma Lazarus - Statue of Liberty National Monument (U.S. National Park Service). (2016). Nps.gov. https://www.nps.gov/stli/learn/historyculture/emma-lazarus.htm
Ganz, M. (2016). *What is public narrative?* Harvard College. https://dash.harvard.edu/server/api/core/bitstreams/7312037d-c817-6bd4-e053-0100007fdf3b/content

Brown, A. M. (2017). *Emergent strategy*. AK Press.

Mitchell, K. L. (2019). *Experience inquiry: 5 powerful strategies, 50 practical experiences*. Corwin.

Morales, R. (2025). *The soil is more important*. https://www.rlmartstudio.com/wp-content/uploads/05-Soil-More-Important-Than-Seeds-web.pdf

Orr, D. W. (2004). *Earth in mind: On education, environment, and the human prospect*. (pp. 7–15). Island Press.

Rothstein, R. (2017). *The color of law: A forgotten history of how our government segregated America*. Liveright Publishing Corporation.

Sobel, D. (2004). *Place-based education: Connecting classrooms and communities*. Orion.

Sobel, D. (2008). *Childhood and nature: Design principles for educators*. Stenhouse Publishers.

3

Agitate, Agitate, Agitate

Getting Stuck in the Mud

One day, I was mapping a particularly muddy area next to our school with students. A few students had on rain boots that allowed them to go deeper into the mud. The swishing and squelching suctioning sound of the mud with each footstep was irresistible. The deeper you moved into the mud, the harder it became to keep taking steps, but the challenge of moving under the growing pressure of the mud made for an adventure.

Finally, the end of class was approaching. I blew my whistle to let everyone know it was time to meet up and head in. Nearly everyone joined up—at which point we heard one boy call out, "I'm stuck in the mud!" I quickly moved to his side and saw that the mud had reached the very top of his boots. I gave him my hand and helped him get himself unstuck. As we walked in, he told me that he had just gone a little too far. I was happy that he was able to realize it and relieved that he was okay.

Sometimes, we have to risk getting stuck in the mud to be able to learn to trust ourselves, our bodies and one another. It's only when we do get stuck, and then reflect on it, that we come to see that learning to listen to our bodies and one another can both help us from getting stuck in the first place and help us in getting unstuck.

Reflection Questions

How are we affected by the people and places around us? How do we develop the trust that we need to explore unknowns, these learning edges?

A student explores the muddy stream by our school.

We need to playfully work with students to hone our questions, our understanding of problems and to keep moving our learning forward.

The difference between the world as it is and the world as it should be must be continuously brought to the forefront of our minds and must be felt as a steady beat in our hearts. When we forget the world as it could be, we sink into cynicism. Mitigating cynicism requires the teacher-as-organizer to practice agitation.

Agitation is a way to remind of the shortcomings of the way things are and to inspire people to take a step toward the way things could be. And after we have taken one step toward the way things could be, agitation reminds us that one step is not enough and that we should take another and another.

Absent agitation, the status quo prevails. It is invisible and unnamed. The status quo is invisible and unnamed because it is "just the way things are and have always been". Agitation gives us all—teachers, students, colleagues—the opportunity to claim our own agency when otherwise we might be rocked to sleep by the promoters of passivity.

So how do we teachers agitate? Is agitation aggressive or mean? When do we agitate?

Noticing the Unexpected in the Every Day

Building our civic muscle requires learning how to find common ground. Finding common ground can start with the little patch of land right under your feet. It may be grass, cement or gravel under our feet, but that little piece of ground connects us to common experiences in our area. We can start to see this when we use a place-based learning framework. Our ability to tune into our senses, which was discussed in Chapter 1, is a starting point. I would like to suggest that we must also learn to be agitated by the common places in our life.

Taking notice is a form of being agitated by the common places in our lives. Being agitated doesn't mean being angry or upset, but rather that we feel the living, breathing nature of the world—and are willing to be affected by it, to be changed by it—and to act in relationship with others. We need to ask questions about our agitation and learning. Sometimes questions lead to more questions and more learning. Other times it leads us toward collective action and change. Openness to being affected by our surroundings puts us in a posture of being changed by agitation, being alive to the situations and circumstances that define the place where we live and learn.

The common places that we visit each day have a special value because they are where we spend the waking hours of our lives. We return to them time and again for many reasons. Among these reasons, we return to learn more about the places and ourselves. These places teach us the importance of being affected by our surroundings and of using our senses to be more effective in our learning.

Confronting "Don't Rock the Boat" Culture

Teaching like an organizer can result in people telling us to "not rock the boat". We are told "don't rock the boat" for the very reason the status quo is unnamed. If we can't name the existing power structure and dynamic, there is nothing to change. Power will continue to operate uninterrupted in the way it has always operated. To name the status quo is an act of agitation. Not only is it an act of agitation, but it is the beginning of rocking the boat and creating a new dynamic that invites plurality of power and more democratic possibilities within the community.

Organizers must unlearn what many of us are taught at an early age: "don't rock the boat". We have been taught through this saying that stability is to be valued above all else. What I would like to suggest is that stability is valuable, but that it holds no special or intrinsic value alone. Stability for stability's sake is not a justification for maintaining things as they are. Instead, we need to assess the costs and benefits of stability, who benefits from it and if there are people who have been bearing undue costs as a result of it. Weighing stability against other values helps us to determine when and how much to rock the boat. It helps us to take measure of the external factors surrounding our decision. Are the waters currently choppy? Is there a risk of capsizing? No one factor or value outweighs others and when we learn that, we are placed in the position of practicing our decision-making skills—we are captains of our destiny.

As captains of our own destiny, we should use the various maps that we have created (in Chapter 2) to set our course for navigation. Along these lines, we can consider when we need to use varied tactics.

Holding steady can be a tactic. We can use the tactic of holding steady to buy time when we don't possess the power that we need to change a situation. This conserves our energy. We can try to wait for conditions to change by conserving our energy.

In contrast, expending our energy (and resources) when we feel like it won't change the conditions of our circumstances can lead to exhaustion. We forgo future energy use when we are continuously exhausted. While we look calm on the surface, a frenetic pace where we are continuously treading water under the surface leads us to a point of exhaustion that increases the likelihood of making poor decisions. Learning to be in touch with your head (analyze the situation), your heart (feel your emotions) and your gut (use your instincts) teaches us when and how to agitate for change. Nobody knows your body like you—which means you and the people you are in community with have an advantage in making change when you learn to trust yourself and each person in turn learns to trust themselves—creating a collective body of knowledge for teaching, learning and organizing.

Time as Agitational Tool

Tempo is a tactic. This is true in the classroom. I can think of many times when I felt out of sync with a class. Maybe I was pushing the pace of a project or maybe it felt like an activity was dragging on for too long. Each of these feelings is an example of how tempo is a tactic. Our goal as teachers is to use the organizer lens to see how time can be used to create a rhythm for creation, creativity and self-direction within the classroom.

You can pause time when you teach like an organizer. This is the magic of co-creating a powerful narrative with students. The draw to pretend brings students to be lost in the minutes of the class. This happens when we create ancient Egyptian escape rooms in class. Students get so lost in the world of tombs and ancient riddles that when I call them back to the world of the living, they ask, "How can class already be over? We just started!" and "Can we have a few more minutes, please?"

Time is an agitational force. It brings contrast between the tasks that we want to get lost in and the tasks that feel like a ripcurrent—where we struggle to keep from being wholly subsumed, but come to realize that struggling against the waves only hastens our demise. As teachers, we have to know the patterns of ripcurrents, both for ourselves and for our students. Often, they are related to interpersonal issues and the challenges that accompany learning independence. Classrooms where students can learn through social activities can be a mitigating factor for some interpersonal issues—as students who know there is a social aspect of the learning can be more willing to participate in a way that can increase their standing among peers.

Scatterplot Opinions

Time can help to structure social interaction in the class by creating a tempo. One simple structured sequence that I use is to provide a prompt that requires students to evaluate a claim or evidence. Students will read the prompt and write down whether they strongly agree, agree, disagree or strongly disagree with the prompt.

Once everyone has a chance to review all the prompts, we will create a human scatterplot by laying down two large pieces of tape on the floor to create two giant axes (an alternative version of this activity can be done with sticky notes). The horizontal x-axis will range from "strongly agree" to "strongly disagree". The y-axis will range from "not so important" to "very important". I will read the prompt out aloud and then ask students to find where they fall on the scatterplot. Once in place, I ask students to look around and see where they and their peers fall. I will try to keep the conversation and the students moving, keeping each discussion point to two minutes. The sequence can be: read the prompt, ask why are you standing where you are (trying to get a sample of the various positions students have taken), listen for the students to explain their position and move to the next person before finishing by asking what trends students noticed. Then, read the next prompt and repeat the cycle.

One element that is built into this activity is a kind of double assessment. Students need to think about their opinion in the form of taking a position on whether they agree or disagree with the given prompt, but then they must also assess whether they think the prompt and their opinion are really relevant to the overall topic of the day. This can lead to students having a strong opinion on a topic but feeling like the prompt wasn't so important. On the other hand, students can take a position of strongly disagreeing with a topic but feel that the prompt is very important. This double evaluation gets students to weigh their opinion while considering the relevance of their opinion (and the prompt) to the community. It's an activity primed for agitational discovery and having students reconsider their positions through coming face to face with varied viewpoints.

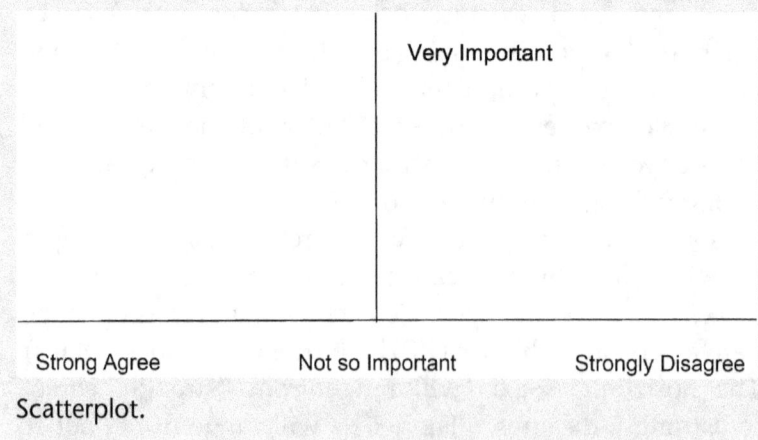

Scatterplot.

It can be tempting to think of tempo as a tactic only of structure and restraint. This limitation of our use of the tool of tempo could very well be a byproduct of the system that most schools work within where we have 50-ish minutes of time per day with each class of students. In this system, time is always short and tempo can easily force a march through our lessons. When time is short, as it often is, activities like the scatterplot discussion, mentioned above, hold particular value because they embody the agitational idea of "shaking things up"—to bring new ideas to the surface. Each statement we read together, each time we listen to a peer express his/her opinion and each time we relocate to a different point on the scatterplot, we are "shaking things up"— closely examining what we have found and then allowing things to settle before we repeat the process. This process has a rhythm and as the teacher, we need to feel that rhythm and also how the class is responding to it.

There is also a relationship between tempo and depth as agitational tactics. The depth and scope of the agitation will be constrained by the time limitations we impose on our activities. If we constantly use highly structured activities—we will often "scoop up" similar ideas. If we constantly lack structure—we may sink into the morass of murky philosophizing. This is to say that our awareness of tempo can help us in determining with our classes the next thing to try. It can be helpful to sink into the depths of a topic when students think things are too cut and dry. It can also be helpful to use a structured activity to pinpoint misconceptions.

Develop your feel and check in with the class—asking them: would it help to try something new out? Sometimes I'll hear the response of the class and I understand their words and body language to mean something other than exactly what they said. They might say, "No, we're good". When I ask them if they want to try something new. But, what I understand them to be saying is, "We are comfortable where we are and that comfort is keeping us satisfied with things as they are right now". My next move has to both acknowledge their response and fit with my teacher's gut. This can mean that I respond, "Okay, let's use the last fifteen minutes to keep working on our project". It can also sound like, "I hear that you're all feeling like it's crunch time on this project. It's true that we only have a day left to wrap it up. But for that reason, I think it's important we try something new to double check your understanding of some key ideas. That way you'll be sure the final product is just the way you want it". There is no "always right answer" or response, which is why we, as teachers, need to keep in touch with our gut.

Place as Agitational Force

It can take time for interest to develop. Sometimes an idea can be like a pebble in our shoe. We don't really notice it after first, but it's bouncing around, rubbing up against different parts of our foot. Before we know it, either we get a blister or we have to take the shoe off and shake it out. The terrain that we walk will have a direct impact on the amount of pebbles that we may get in our shoes. If we walk only on cement sidewalks, we will get fewer pebbles than if we are walking on gravel roads. Our experience with these different surfaces can change the way we walk and influence where we walk. As organizers, we have to both give the time for interests to develop and be ready to mix things up. What we don't want to do is to just leave the pebble in our shoe, or even worse, avoid all areas that might put pebbles in our shoe in the first place!

The smallest of interactions has the potential to awaken in us great curiosity. When we have encounters with the world that stick with us, it is because there is something stirring within us. This stirring may be the sign of a latent interest starting to emerge or it could be an element of the self trying to be recognized. In either case, we can do well to listen to how we are being moved and what it is that moves us. We need to stay curious when we face uncertainty. Agitation is very much about being able to reach down into the unknown and examine whatever it is that you can bring forth. Adopting this mindset as a teacher opens us to model curiosity for our students. This is especially important for students who have not experienced place as an agitational force for curiosity in their lives—or at least not in a continuous and intentional way.

What's down there?

I had shut the gate on my way out after a daylong visit to a school in Berlin, Germany. It had been a full day of observing students and teachers. Turning and heading toward the nearest metro stop, I was struck by a vision of exactly what I hadn't known that I was looking for. It was a child peering underneath a construction gate. He was trying to get a clear view of a backhoe at work. The boy pressed his body to the cement slabs of the sidewalk, determined to see the jolting, scooping and lifting of the large yellow machine. His mother, standing by, looked at me with a twinkle in her eyes. She saw the magical effect of place on her son. She saw how digging down into the earth generated intrigue and wonder. The moving of brick, dirt and remnants of an old building moved her son.

Years later, I think back to this moment and think about the many lessons it holds for me as a teacher. Most of all, it

Photo: What's down there? Outside a school in Berlin, Germany.

> has made me consider the hidden world that is plainly in sight all around us—and our deep motivation to take what is hidden and make it seen, to create adventures out of the mundane.

As teachers, I'm sure we can each think of the most mundane of topics and lessons that we must cover. In the geography classroom, one topic that I had long felt fell into this generally boring category was the concept of location. The textbook tells us that location has two forms: relative and absolute. Relative location can be thought of as using landmarks as reference points for getting around. Absolution location is all about precise coordinates—think the global positioning system (GPS) that our cell phones use or the latitude and longitude coordinates that we see drawn on maps and globes.

Again, we can reflect on the organizing idea of the idealized vision of what learning could be and the real-world setting where we teach each day. Take our real-world teaching situations, the imperfect areas around our schools, the standards, etc. Apply the learning principles of Sobel (2008) to create an agitational organizing dynamic and together, we can motivate students to really get into their learning. The appeal of Sobel's learning principles drives learning in the real world. Students can't help but to be motivated by the agitational gap of the "world as it is" and the "world as it should be" when we approach learning like an adventure.

After thinking back to the boy who was peering through the fence to catch a look at the backhoe, I decided to try to weave in the agitational concept of digging down to uncover new truth. "How could we take these ideas to create a concrete experience for students?" I wondered. Then, it hit me, archeologists and paleontologists use grid systems when they dig down in search for relics and fossilized remains. From this realization sprang the idea for the unit: Paleolithic Park!

The unit would fulfill the requirement of learning about different kinds of location culminating with the creation of a dig site outside our school. The students would design artifacts and fossils to be placed at the dig sites in a way that could be interpreted by their peers from other groups.

Uncovering the Hidden with a Grid Memory Game

Early on in the unit, I asked students how grids could be used when trying to uncover hidden objects. One boy explained that grids could help us "catalogue" our finds, keeping track of where everything was found with a clear system. With this in mind, I set out to create a game where students could try out the concept of uncovering and cataloguing. For years, I had described using grid systems to students as similar to playing battleship. Even in this digital age, many students still get the reference, "B5, hit and sunk". Since the battleship reference worked, I looked for a life-sized grid that we could use to play on and practice using grid and coordinate systems.

Over the years, I have learned that part of teaching like an organizer is rethinking how we can take what we have and turn it into what we need to get what we want (Chambers & Cowan, 2003). Place-based learning suggests that we look around us to see what lessons might arise from our natural or built environments. If we have a cement walkway and need to learn about grids then we use those two things to get what we want: the knowledge necessary to plan our own Paleolithic dig.

As it happened, the front walkway at our school had cement slabs that were about four feet long by four feet wide—so I took some chalk before school and made a makeshift grid system. I numbered the y-axis 1–5 and lettered the x-axis a–v, making an enormous playing field. I then printed pairs of pictures relating to Paleolithic times on paper. We mixed up the papers and placed each face down—one per cement slab with a small cone on top to make sure the papers wouldn't blow away. Lastly, I let students pick their own teams of 4–5 students to work with in the activity.

I provided the students with a clipboard and blank paper copy of the grid. I shared the rules of the game as teams spread out along the x-axis. Each team had a chance to say two coordinates and flip over the corresponding papers. The team with the most matches at the end was the winner. Students talked with their teammates and strategized about which papers to flip over throughout the game. Using the grid system outside was a stepping stone for students that gave them a visible idea of how a coordinate system could be created out of anything. Flipping the images over in the game also paralleled the idea of digging down and examining something that was once hidden.

Sifting through Plans, Materials and Jobs
In the next class, I wanted to guide the students toward using the memory grid game as a scaffold for applying grid systems to our Paleolithic adventure. This meant bringing to mind planning questions that could help students take more ownership of the work. I first showed the class a video that demonstrated what a dig site looked like and how the paleontologists approached preparing for the dig and what the dig site looked like as the project progressed. I then posed to the class three preparation questions and handed out three sticky notes of three different colors to each student in the class. I wrote the three preparation questions on big pieces of paper and invited students to write their own responses on their sticky notes before discussing one of their notes and sticking each to its matching question. The questions, which I believe all have flexible roots that could be used for many different projects, were: (1) What materials would we need for an excavation? (2) What jobs could students do to create and lead an excavation? (3) What story could our excavation tell? Again, I was thinking back to the organizing mindset of: take what we have to get what we need to get what we want. If we wanted to have a fun and adventurous excavation we needed materials and for everyone to do their chosen jobs—and this meant taking our plan and putting it into action.

I narrowed down the major jobs identified by the students into four categories: artists, guides, writers and designers. Artists created artifacts from the Paleolithic era. Writers created a background story calling the adventurers to action. Guides designed maps using landmarks to navigate adventurers to the dig site. Designers worked with the other three partners to plan the placement of the various artifacts at the dig site. The designer would also prepare the dig site, which meant clearing away debris, digging down into the earth and eventually guiding the placement of artifacts and covering them.

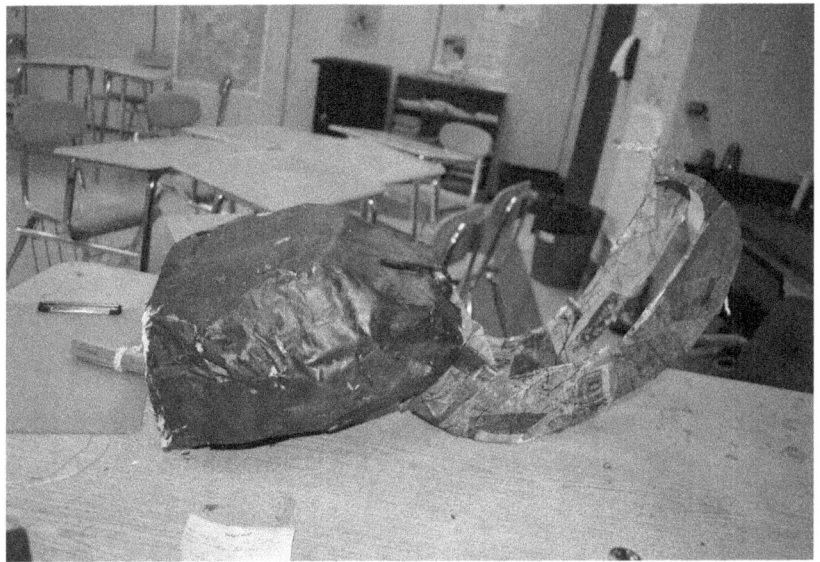

Mammoth skull created by student.

Students started bringing in odds and ends from home—an old paint brush to dust off mammoth bones, newspapers and various other recycled materials. I tracked down other things, like glue, twine and cardboard. Student ingenuity led to the creation of a cardboard frame for a mammoth skull that would later be paper macheted and painted before large cardboard tusks were mounted to it. Another group looked up information on a

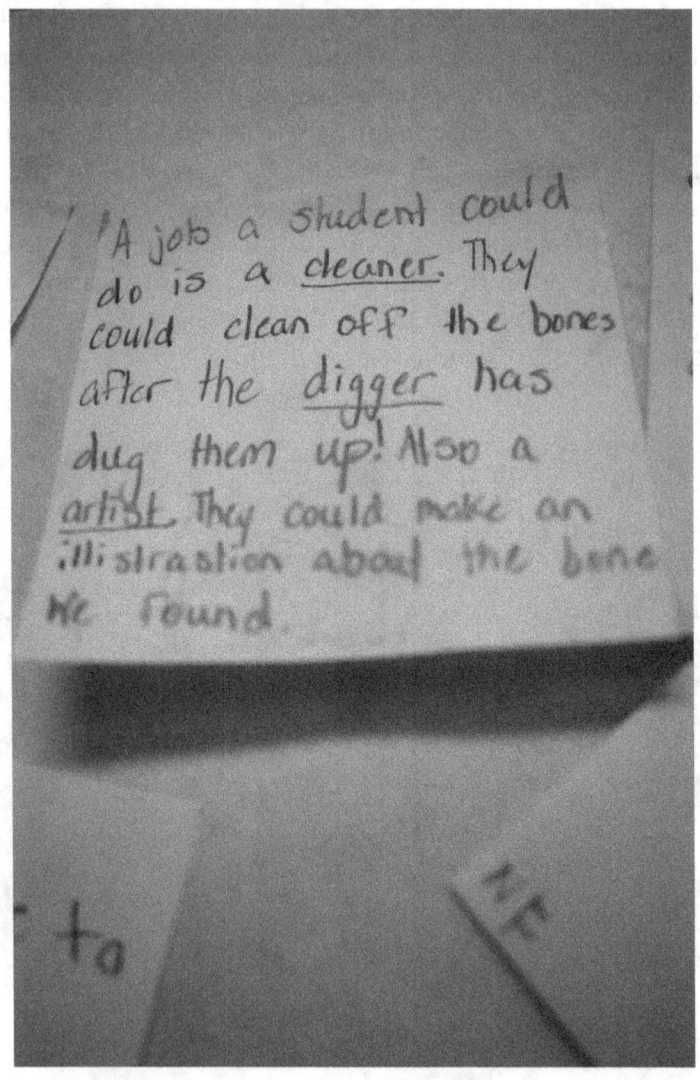

Student sticky note from material brainstorm.

giant prehistoric beaver to use as a model for the creation of their own buck-toothed beaver skull.

The student guides took a last tour of the distance between the classroom and the dig sites to make sure their maps and directions could get the adventurers to the correct location of the dig sites. At the same time, writers and artists worked to finish up their products. Then, each group worked to clear their sites and place their artifacts—covering everything up carefully to conceal the hidden secrets of Paleolithic times.

"Look", I said on the day of the first excavation, "There are many hidden secrets out there in the woods. It may be that some items become lost to history, but it is your job to recover and record as many artifacts as you can, listening to your guides and the site experts. Good luck!" With that, I turned things over to the guides, who handed their navigational maps off to the adventurers that they had been paired with.

One team of adventurers made their way down to the woods using the prepared map, only to find a peer who was acting as a site expert, who greeted them with an enthusiastic:

> Congratulations–you've made it to an important place. Here, a group of stone age Homo Sapiens and Woolly Mammoths were thriving in the wilderness until they needed to seek shelter. They found a cave to stay the night, but suddenly, the cave shut, trapping them. They tried to get out, but the rocks blocked the door. Hours went by and then days. The days changed to weeks and weeks changed to months...until there was nothing left. Your journey begins exploring the forest and excavating the remains of the Homo Sapiens and Mammoths in the cave...The long lost mysteries of the Stone Age will be revealed!. Welcome ... to Paleolithic Park!

With that, the site experts spontaneously hummed the theme song from Jurassic Park and the team of adventurers designated one member of their group to gently move debris away from the site in search of a sign of the mammoths. Other team members stood ready to record any found artifacts by sketching on the blank coordinate plane that I had provided them.

Student at the dig site.

In our post-excavation reflections, students described the excavation and documentation process, where artifacts were located on their grid systems and what story they thought the scene may tell based on the orientation of the artifacts. We discussed how in their enthusiasm, some students brush away leaves, dirt and sticks too vigorously, damaging an artifact or displacing the artifact from its resting place.

For me, the activity came to reaffirm the effectiveness of a steady approach to teaching. We know there will be times when emotion runs high among the students. Our own self-knowledge can help us ground them in learning while hearing what they need from us. We know students will rush and will make mistakes along the way. Our anticipation and explanation of this is an expression of our understanding of the students—what organizers call inoculation. Telling students the common mistakes of any work can reduce their anxiety and prepare them for disappointment and to persevere.

Agitation takes this steady process of digging, examining, charting and planning. If we are to learn new things about ourselves and learn how to work better together, we will find a patient pace that affords our students to learn to make their way through all kinds of obstacles. As teachers, we can be adaptable when we release ourselves from the invisible routines of unspoken expectations and culture—when we break through the superficial to encourage our students to look for adventure and nuisance in the common places that shape their lives.

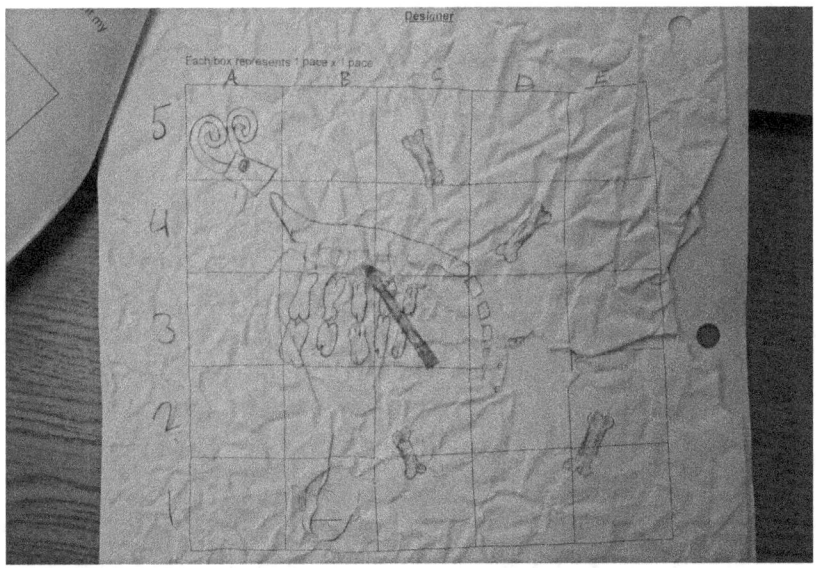

Student excavation site sketch.

How Do We Develop a "Feel" for the Unexpected? The Potentially Agitational Moment

We can get a better feel for the unexpected around our school by coming into relationship with the land and community by our schools. The more we know the literal lay of the land the more we can anticipate what might attract student interest.

My wife worked at one elementary school right on the ocean. New debris constantly washes ashore. She knows that the children she teaches enjoy using the flotsam and jetsam in their lessons and play. While she doesn't know what will arrive on a given day or if that something will ignite the imaginations of the children, she is ready to receive the ocean's gifts each day; being ready is understanding the ebb and flow of teaching, of interests and of ideas. There is a non-permanence to this mindset and it encourages a very practical understanding of the present moment. She acknowledges that there will be slow moments where it feels like the class is slogging through the muddiest of mud flats and there will be fast moments when the class is filled with exuberance and joyousness. As the teacher, we seek to find these moments and use them to open students to the world as it is and the world as it could be.

The Giant's Blue Soap

On a recent morning, a small group of fourth grade students walked the shoreline. Nearby, seagulls strutted along the mud flats, pecking and hunting for morning meals. Then they found it. The bright blue color stood out against the autumn hues of fallen leaves and bare bushes and trees. It was a giant piece of styrofoam. The boys closed in on it quickly, like gulls finding a treasure beneath the mud.

First, they sat on it. It was soft and large enough for three friends to share. Then, they too started to peck and pry. Using their pencils, they tested the depth and hardness of their new-found prize. The foam squeaked and eked as it was prodded, eventually finding relief when the end of class call summoned the boys back to the school.

The styrofoam's solitude was short-lived. A first grade girl was on the move. Her eyes searched the shoreline as she moved with purpose toward the object, which she could not identify with certainty. She embraced it. Wrapping her arms around the block-like mass, she found it to be light for its size. With a combination of awkwardness and ease, she hoisted it up and walked slowly back to the class meeting spot.

"What is it?" asked her teacher.

The little girl paused, unsure of how to answer. Then, she replied, "I think it's a bar of soap. It's a big blue bar of soap. It's a giant's big blue bar of soap".

And with that, the styrofoam had changed from something on the periphery of learning to the centerpiece of learning. As students drifted in and out of the center of the outdoor classroom, they noticed the blue man-made item. Not only that, but it became a kind of shrine to imagination. One boy brought a bone fragment that he found and placed it on the blue block. A little girl brought a dead crab. Another youngster gently placed a little green leaf on it—or as he said, "the last green leaf of the year".

At the end of class, students gathered around the found objects to take inventory. And at that point, some in the class shared that the blue block had a name: styrofoam. This, however, was a minor detail to the children who instead came to an agreement on what it was really—*a museum.*

One of the great questions of teaching is: when to insert oneself into the world of learning?

The case of the giant's big blue bar of soap illustrates how openness to the world creates learning opportunities. These are serendipitous encounters from the children's view, but they are not possible without the organizer mindset and openness of the teacher. Students find new items, like the blue foam block, and they have questions, create stories, participate through play and invite the teacher to draw connections that can illuminate their learning.

> The places around our classrooms become the most essential ingredient in learning as they bring the learning to life. Student discovery of the blue block led to play, which in the end, brought students to want to create a "museum of place". Displaying and discussing the found objects of the schoolyard brought the students to have a common understanding of the shared space, placing them in dialogue with one another about the meaning and relevance of each item. This exemplifies how what we find on the ground can help us organize for common ground.

Accessing Insight and Agitation

The teacher-as-organizer must, above all things, have faith in the people—the students. We must have faith in the students that they are capable of finding problems, sorting them out and working toward solutions. Why do we have to have this kind of faith in students? Without this kind of faith in young people, and people in general, we will be recreating the kinds of relationships based on domination that have been central to our world having so much sorrow, pain and suffering. Our mindset allows us to meet our students where they are—to scaffold learning experiences—and also to believe that each student is capable of taking the next step and the next step and the next step toward understanding themselves, their community and what it would take to improve things bit by bit and day by day. Deeply rooted faith in the potential of young people calls the teacher-as-organizer into action.

Believing in young people calls us to trust young people. We know that the answers to problems that exist are within the students—so we trust that the students, with guidance (and agitation), will be able to surface the answers. This concept of education as awakening the inner self, as bringing something that exists within us out into the world, is a classical concept of education that was popular with the ancient Greeks. Education's epistemological origin in Greek is "to call forth". The educator-as-organizer is a part of this long-held tradition of trusting the student to become what they are meant to be when engaging with work that "calls forth" their inner selves, their true selves. When we trust in the true self of the student, we are opening our classrooms to the "insight" of the students.

Insight or inner knowledge is accessed through different means at different ages. As educators, we create the space where students feel that they can start to go inward to be able to express in community how they really feel and think. We continuously try to know our students, seeing students change and develop as members of the classroom and extended community throughout our time with them. It is in this dynamic of growth and change that we live as teachers as we learn to anticipate the shifting needs of individuals and the group.

What Approaches to Agitation Bring About Insight?

While there are many approaches to teaching as an organizer, let's focus on two complementary approaches, the dove and the fox. I see these as complementary approaches rather than opposites because they both have their times and uses. It's important not to be trapped in just one approach—the teacher-as-organizer must be able to have range to adjust to the needs of the group of students they are working with. Those needs, as we know, change throughout our time with students.

Approach	*Characteristics*	*Works best for …*	*Watch out for …*
The Dove	Soothing, affirming, steadiness	A new group, a group that is coming out of conflict, setting a tone of seriousness, taking on a serious topic or event, entering a time of reflection	Overusing this approach as it may result in students becoming complacent or disinterested.
The Fox	Playful, "trickster", hinting at a bigger picture	A group that is feeling playful or needs to "change things up", drawing attention to nuisance or new paths for learning	This approach becomes overly taxing on the teacher. Use your energy wisely as you alert students to new mysteries and nuisances.

Author and educator Parker Palmer (1998/2017) described the inner self as being like a wild animal. Like a wild animal, the inner self cannot be approached directly. Instead, to get close, you have to walk cautiously and purposefully so as not to scare it away. In practice, this means using parallel stories and metaphors to help students to think about issues. This can help to create the kind of space students need to "step back" and have the kind of perspective that allows for them to really access their thoughts and feelings. Otherwise, the pressing nature of a topic can just be too much, making it difficult to gain insight. The technique of using parallel stories and metaphors is just one way to create the distance teachers as organizers need to cultivate for an insightful learning community.

When We Agitate, We Are Listening to Show Curiosity and Unearth Curiosity?

To agitate is to act. And each action we take when we teach like an organizer is met with a reaction. I've had ideas for lessons that have been met with blank stares. That's a reaction! And it's a reaction that taught me something right away—do something else!

We know that student reactions will be based on so many different factors–and it is our job to figure out what the "secret sauce" is for the learners who we work with each day. We do know that building community and unearthing curiosity as a teacher-as-organizer requires that we develop keen detection skills—that we be seismologists of engagement. We approach each day with our ear to the ground as we try to judge: What kind of reaction did our provocation summon? What are the on-ramps and invitations to participate for learners? Reflecting on our provocations allows us to tune our approach to helping students to learn toward the common good.

Along the way, we slowly learn about ourselves as teachers and organizers. One way or another, we develop our own habits, go-to styles in our lessons and classroom affect. It took me a long time to find out I can vacillate between being over the top enthusiastic and being a quiet listener. Recognizing these tendencies has allowed me to work toward making adjustments as I read the room, act and react. I have learned that there are going to be times when I misjudge the mood in the classroom or when a lesson works with one class and doesn't click with the next group. So, I stay curious about my practice, try to generate more positive energy by finding wins and try not to beat myself up.

When We Tell v. When We Trust

Debrah Meier (1995) famously said that "teaching is listening and learning is talking". The same could be said for organizing. When we listen, the next step becomes clear. We know if we need to reinforce a concept or idea or if it's time to move on. We learn if we need to move to a more structured activity or if it's time for students to take on more responsibility. All this comes from our ability to be in tune with our class.

Some of my teaching friends state their observations to the class to help the class decide the next step. Others pose questions, asking the class to check-in on their bodies and minds. These approaches are fairly typical ways for students to self-assess how things are going and to take note of their individual feelings while being reminded of how their feelings fit within the mosaic of the classroom community.

I have observed and taught in classrooms where students have full trust in the teacher to make the call about what's coming next. In my experience, this is more common. Yet, even when we practice this way of being together in the classroom, I try to use little clues as a way of agitating and generating curiosity. And to me, that's an essential part of agitation, it's about bringing about a question where otherwise there would not be one.

Competition as Agitation

Yes, it's okay to use competition in the classroom. It's a tactic that can bring about joy, frustration and a whole range of different emotions. Competition can be demotivating at times too. Most of the competitions that we play in class are team-based and encourage teams to work together, to communicate and to find out the different interests and talents of classmates. We should use competition as a tool of agitation, engagement and learning in the classroom based on knowing our students. We need to know who needs what kind of support and we need to have the mindset that we need to be building toward a community where we can support one another, whatever the outcome of the competition may be.

Current Event Notecards: A Low-Stakes Competition for Initial Engagement

Direction: Give each student an index card. Create a digital bank of students-friendly news sites or use a resource like a Scholastic Magazine. Ask students to read a news article. After reading the article, have them write a one-sentence summary of the article, followed by a factual question that has a "point to it" answer in the text of the article. In my class, "point to it" means they literally have to be able to point to the answer. Students should write the answer down on the back of their index card. Collect all the cards. Make teams of 4–5 students. Each team gets a small white board, expo marker and eraser. Use the student generated cards to play the "Current Event Notecard Game". Read a student's summary and question and each group should write their best guess for the answer on their white board. Ten points are awarded per correct answer and every team has a chance to earn points.

You can also ask students to cite their source when writing the cards. In sixth grade, I usually ask for the title of the article and the first and last name of the author to be included at the bottom of the card.

Take-away: Agitation should be fun. What's not fun? Well, much of the news these days isn't fun at all! Yet, we can use competition to get kids interested in the news and get them reading. One middle school friendly site that students have enjoyed for news for years has been DogoNews. Colleagues have also used sites like NEWSELA.com, which has leveled texts that can help with students access "just right" reading levels.

Credit: I was first taught this game by Valerie Wolfson, a teacher with over two decades of experience of Oyster River Middle School, Durham, New Hampshire (NH).

Moving the Unmoved and How Competition Can Create FOMO

When we consider how we are helping students to move toward becoming their best selves, we can see all the different tools at our disposal. Fear of missing out (FOMO) is an element of competition that we as teachers should be aware of. Competition can create the perception of "winners" and "losers" and being a "winner" can be a powerful motivator for someone of any age. We don't want to be "left out" of "being a winner". This fear, in turn, can drive participation.

It's important to pause and reflect with students about these feelings, exploring what drives them, and how classroom games can teach us broader lessons about our communities and societies. Reflection questions may scaffold up from specifics about a particular lesson or game to more general and open-ended questions that invite deeper analytical thinking. Like many teachers, I've struggled with competition over the years, especially in the years of political polarization and the post-COVID teaching era of today. Where I've landed (for now) is that competition can be joyous for students and can help students to build resilience and a sense of criticality. If we ignore the benefits of competition in the classroom, students are still going to experience the downsides of competition outside of school, yet often without the support of a teacher and most likely without ever pausing for analysis and reflection.

Competition has a way of moving those who would otherwise not be moved. To teach like an organizer, we are looking at the real-world fact that there will be a wide range of motivations in our classroom. Knowing our students allows us to use competition in a positive way that creates a supportive atmosphere where students are invited into the game of competition.

The Thermometer

Organizers and teachers know there are times when we need to "turn up the heat" or "cool things down". We have an eye on the group's "thermometer" and try to make the adjustments needed to optimize our team's growth. We've learned through trial and error that too much intensity when it comes to schoolwork, or any kind of work, leads to burnout and folks becoming less responsive. We have also figured out that growth is a kind of progress and progress requires forward motion. Forward motion will create friction and friction will create heat.

We must make progress to keep the vision of the world as it could be alive. Without progress we deflate, go into hibernation or lose hope. In the classroom, progress means students growing and stretching their abilities to be self-directed, to know themselves and their community and to communicate their needs, ideas, questions and findings.

The thermometer tool is one way that we can visualize progress. Providing students with a tool to visual progress gives them the ability to check in with themselves and with peers—providing collective ownership of the classwork and the classroom.

At the base of the thermometer are the "low" temperature activities that are indicators for our goals. We see "higher" temperature activities and topics as we move up the thermometer. These "high temperature" activities and topics are the activities that take time and practice to achieve. The thermometer tool is a symbol of the saying that "progress is made at the speed of trust". In other words, we can't move toward the high temperature activities and topics if we lack the basic trust at the lower levels of heat. In our polarized times, we know that "heated" exchanges can be detrimental to the community when we haven't done the relational work necessary to prepare for difficult exchanges.

When we work with students to improve communal civic life, a low temperature activity might be describing our likes and dislikes or hobbies. The next level up can include starting to develop reciprocal relationships with our classmates and sharing about ourselves and our interests. Continuing up the thermometer, we are looking to go beyond the superficial and understand some of the conflicts that exist within our community. At the top of our thermometer we look to finding resolution for the conflicts and challenges that we face.

Communication is an essential skill that we can track by "reading the thermometer". A debate is a heated classroom activity, in that many debates are adversarial in structure. One side will win and one side will lose. It is helpful to practice other forms of dialogue and discussion, prior to jumping into the more adversarial style debate. This way, we are building relational trust among students and showing students that by sustaining dialogue we can learn from one another. This isn't to dismiss the value of debate, which can be immense, but rather to prepare students to eventually reap the full benefits of debate rather than getting stuck in the "us versus them" dynamic that can underlie debate.

We should be aware of the convergence of "heated topics" and "heated activities". Working our way through the progression of heated activities before taking on heated topics in our activities can be an effective strategy for building classroom capacity. Students can experience success with the varied levels of heated dialogue, including working through adversarial exchanges and see the results with fun topics. After seeing what works, as well as the challenges of different styles of activities, students can take on more "heated topics".

Our end goal is to afford students the chance to experience learning from "turning up the heat". To do this, they need to reflect on their own comfort levels. After an activity, we can ask our students to consider where we are as a class in in terms of the scale of the thermometer. We can follow up with ideas for responsive next steps. Do we need to turn down the heat or turn it up? What is the next best move for us as we try to learn and grow together?

Reclaiming common ground and rebuilding our civic space require that students experience building trust as individuals and as a group, honoring diverse voices and working through conflict. When we teach like an organizer, we slowly decipher the next best step that the class can take based on our observations of the last moves that we've made. We are determining with the class the readiness for the next level of "heat" or if we need to hold steady to reestablish trust. Seeking steadiness is a move that allows us to regain our footing before we make our next move, our next attempt at progress.

Change Requires Friction and Friction Creates Heat—A Good Teacher and Organizer Knows When to Turn Up or Turn Down the Heat

One summer, I was working with a group of students in Berkeley, CA. Our class was composed of students from places as far away as Shanghai and Bermuda. We traveled around the Bay Area participating in various forms of service learning alongside residents and nonprofit staff members. This was a big deal for the teenagers who I was working with—for some it was one of the first semi-independent trips of their lives. Knowing this, we understood that some students would be coming with heightened emotions and a desire to seem invulnerable to their new peers.

In our first few days, it was apparent that one student from Albania was isolating herself from her peers. She claimed to have nothing to learn from the homeowners who spoke to us about the rush of tech money that was rapidly turning over established working class neighborhoods. She had no use for helping to restock the shelves at a food pantry or learning about the effects of food insecurity. Albania, she asserted, had no problems. In her mind, there was clearly nothing to learn in Berkeley and her time would have been much better spent at the mall.

This was hard to hear for her peers. They made connections between our site work each day and life in their home communities. The declarative statement of the one student from Albania felt like a denial of the shared experiences at our daily site visits. A challenging dynamic for any educator!

We continued to talk to one another, finding out more about one another.

One day, surrounded by a chain link fence, we weeded a community garden. "This is nothing compared to the gardens in Albania", our struggling student made clear throughout the day. We heard her. Our guides to the garden told us about the neighborhood. Hard metals from decades ago made it impossible to plant directly in the soil, which was why the garden was composed entirely of raised beds.

The rote cycle of weeding was rhythmic. Searching for where weeds met the ground with our hands, pulling them out, shaking off the dry dirt, throwing the weeds in a pile headed for the compost and repeating. Conversation eased— we just did the work. When the pile of weeds grew too high, a student brought a pitchfork and scooped up the wanton greens into a wheelbarrow.

Students, like all people, are filled with their own anxieties and insecurities. Sometimes it is a return to the pattern of everyday tasks where our hands are busy that allows us to turn down the heat and stand in the familiar. It is then that we can be at ease, be ourselves and decide when to take the next challenge.

Organizing Stories: LVEJO

Another summer, early in my career as a teacher, I was introduced to a group of young people in Chicago who belong to the Little Village Environmental Justice Organization (LVEJO). These young people had lived in a neighborhood that had one of the highest rates of asthma and emphysema in Chicago. Children were the most affected by these twin attacks on the body, which were caused by the coal burning plant in their backyards. One of the LVEJO youth leaders pointed to a car parked nearby and said, "Before we took action, a car parked on the street at night could accumulate an inch of soot by morning." Slowly, the group worked to build a coalition to address the health and environmental effects of the coal burning plant—eventually the plant was shut down.

I've kept this story with me throughout my time as a teacher, because it shows that organizing for change at scale has been done by young people. Oftentimes those stories of young people moving mountains to bring about lasting change for their communities are not told or are not known outside of their immediate areas. It's the teacher-as-organizer who needs to collect these stories and convey them to other young people to show that it's possible: someone like you has done this and has overcome the various obstacles of the adult-built world to make things better.

Stories from the world of organizing help us to see what is possible. They also help us to see where common mistakes have been made in efforts to improve communities. We can learn from both types of stories. By sharing these stories we can also encourage young people to reflect on their own successes and challenges.

The Balance of Power Assessment

Teaching like an organizer requires that we assess our capacity for agitation. It also requires that we gauge other forces within the community to understand all the interests on any particular issue. We don't want to give students the idea that learning about an issue is all it takes to address an issue. The present state of an issue is often the product of compromises that have been reached between those invested in the issue. To use any of our agitational tools, which help to build interest and awareness, without assessing the current balance of power, could produce unexpected results that run counter to the desired outcome. That is why it can be a useful exercise to use the balance of power assessment (shown below) to determine what kind of action your group might want to take.

Your Power:
What can you do?
What is your capacity?
How can you increase your capacity?

The Opposition's Power:
What will the opposition do?

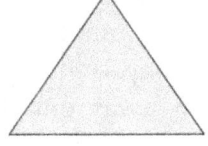

Balance of power assessment

As relayed from Ellen David Friedman

Balance of power assessment.

A balance of power assessment asks a group to determine how their current power measures up to the oppositional power on an issue. The opposition is defined simply as the people who have interests on this issue at this time that are different from our own. This can be a tricky concept to discuss, but a necessary one. I try to emphasize that the opposition is not permanent, that it changes and that someone can be on one side of an issue one day and another side another day. If students are having a difficult time with the concept of opposition, I'll talk with them about how in sports a coach might make new groups to scrimmage for each practice. All the players are really on the same team, but we mix things up to provide everyone a chance to play with one another. "Even if we are never on the same team", I remind them, "we'll high five at the end to show that we all gave it our best effort". Most sixth graders find this to be an acceptable explanation—and they've heard similar things from their parents, families and coaches, which helps the idea of respecting the opposition to resonate.

As we start the balance of power analysis, I'll print out the diagram for each student or group. Next, I ask students to write their issue in the triangle in the middle of the diagram. I ask students to talk about the following questions as a team or class: What can you do? What is your capacity? How can you increase your capacity?

For example, students might be thinking about the issue of litter around the school. We would write this in the center triangle. If it's the first time we've tried this activity, I read each question aloud and ask volunteers to share two or three ideas before giving the groups two minutes to brainstorm a list of responses for the question. They say things like, "we could pick the litter", "we could throw away our trash", "we could hire more custodians" or "we could give a detention to anyone who is caught littering". In this brainstorm phase, I try to suspend judgment and just keep students talking and writing about their ideas.

When I ask "What is your capacity?" students start to think about what might be practical for them. "Well, I have classes all day", one student might regretfully explain, "so I can't be outside picking up litter all day every day". "Only adults can give detentions", another might volunteer. "We have our lunch and little free time after lunch", a last student could point out.

"Okay, moving on to our last question on this side of the scale", I'll transition the class to the third question, "How can you increase your capacity?" This question brings students to generate ideas like: "what if instead of one of us picking up trash, we had all twenty of us working together?" "What if we had a longer lunch?" "We could change the rules of the school to allow a few very responsible students to give out detentions", "We could have a fundraiser to pay for another custodian" or "We could have bigger trash cans". We move on once we have a few different directions we could go to build our capacity to address the issue (and being fully aware that there will be some wayward ideas that will be filtered out by the students).

At this point, I direct students' attention to the question of the opposition and the opposition's power. All of our work to this point will be weighed against the question of what the opposition will do. So, who is the opposition? Are they opposed to any action on the issue? In our example, it might be easy to start with people who are littering and what we could do to address the issue. Would they be against us staying after school to pick up trash one day? Would they be against us picking up trash after lunch each day? How would they react? Students might offer that the litterers might be mad if they are part of the group that must stay after school, they might miss soccer practice. The litterer might just keep littering if other people keep picking up after them. They might stop littering if they know that we get to play more at lunch if everyone picks up two pieces of trash when they are done eating. Starting with a simple action can help us to talk about the more complex actions, in turn helping the class to best determine the course of action.

"Who would be opposed to adding more trash cans and why?" I ask. Students respond: "Custodians because they would have more work to do". "The principal because she would need to add money to the budget to pay for them", "Teachers because we might need to store them in their rooms".

Leading the class further in exploring these views, I probe, "what would they do if they opposed your action?" The students point out: "The custodians might have less time to do their other jobs". "The principal might have less money for pencils". "The teachers might have less room for our backpacks". We could then build out these ideas more to make sure that we have a good idea of the possible pushback from pursuing any of the actions.

The class can then move to assessing the big picture for action. We can now see that some of our actions might result in reactions that we might not like or that might lead to worse problems. We need to also be aware that depending on what action we pick, it may result in more people joining the opposition. Finally, we want to think about our big picture game plan for the issue. We might not resolve the issue all at once—in fact, it's rare to solve an issue so easily. With this in mind, we want to think about our first action choice, how it can help us to grow our capacity and how it can get more people involved in helping to address the problem.

Whatever the group picks, we will have weighed our options and we will be prepared to learn from whatever action we decide to take. In this regard, we can come back and change course or redirect our future efforts based on how things play out in the real world. This is a different approach than a "one and done" mobilization effort, in that we want to be able to grow our capacity for creating sustainable change.

The visual of the balance of power can help students to start to see how change can take time. You need to build capacity to shift things toward your direction on an issue. Otherwise, you might see a tilting of the scale in your direction and then an immediate (and more permanent) reversal of course. The questions about current capacity and building capacity lend themselves to extending our plan for improving how we address the issue. The balance of power model invites students to think about whether the actions we take could build confidence among supporters or if it might be overly agitational for the opponents in such a way that calcifies their position and impedes future change efforts. It's not always easy to tell who stands in opposition to change, which means that our assessment of the balance of power can be strengthened by going out and talking to members of the community about the issues. Again, this links back to essential one-on-one conversations. Changes, of course, are not always zero sum. There are win-win solutions, yet we still need to weigh possible solutions and reactions. We'll next consider another way to think about how our actions can agitate for positive change.

Field of Play

As the balance of power analysis taught us, growing our capacity for change is one of the most significant considerations that we need to take into account. That means we need to be clear-eyed on our assessment of where we stand today and what we think are realistic goals for growing our capacity into the future. The field of play analysis is another visual model for thinking about growth.

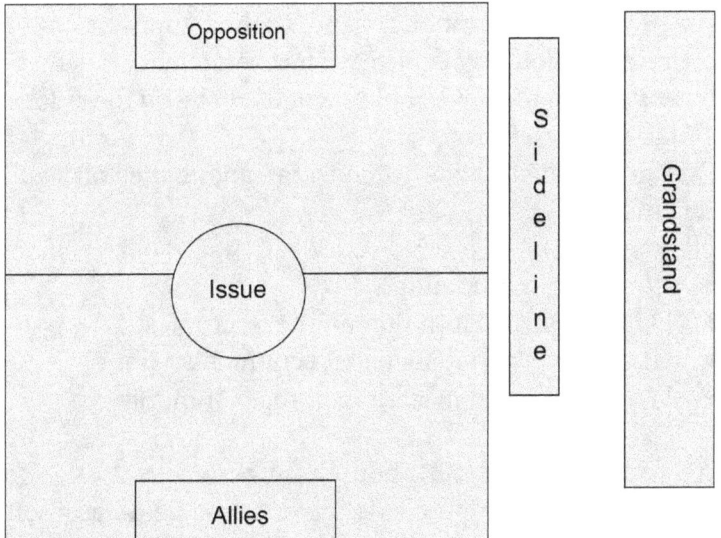

Field of play.

We can start by writing the issue that we are working on in the circle at midfield. I think of the issue as a ball that can move around as we organize around the issue. Most importantly, the field of play model has students consider the all-important factor of people. In this model, I ask students to brainstorm and respond to the following questions to understand the opposition.

- Who is the opposition?
- What are their concerns and what do they have at stake for the issue?
- Who are they connected to in the community?

On the other side of the field, I ask students a similar set of questions about their allies on the issue:

- Who are your allies?
- What are their concerns and what do they have at stake?
- Who are they connected to in the community?

Most importantly to building capacity, we need to think about the people who are on the sideline. Most people are usually uninvolved with public issues, which presents a major opportunity for building capacity. The changemakers who bring more people onto the field of play will likely be on the side of the issue that is successful.

Questions for students to consider about the folks on the sideline include:

- Who is on the sideline?
- Do they have an opinion on the issue?
- Have they previously taken action on an issue?
- Who are they connected to in the community?

We can start to think about how actions we take could bring more people from the sideline onto the field based on the responses that we gather to these questions. If we are unsure about whether our actions will bring more people to the field, we can (and should) track movement as we take action. Even within our class, when students find an issue to work on, it can be helpful to ask: who feels like they are in the grandstand, on the sideline or in the field on this issue? This simple self-assessment can form the basis for reflection at different points in a unit.

The field of play model gets us thinking about how to move folks out of the grandstand and onto the sideline and off the sideline and into the field. Our goal isn't to shift everyone all at once, but to move people toward being a little more engaged with the issue at hand. We must also recognize that people may flow back to the sideline to rest or to prioritize other issues in their lives. This is fine and something that we will talk about more in Chapter 4 where we'll consider timelines for issues. It's a sign that our actions are ineffective or that there are larger factors shifting the issue dynamics if we are noticing more allies leaving the field than entering the field.

The field of play only matters if we have confidence that the issue is one that is deeply felt within the community. The goal is not to move the ball down the field, irrespective of whether the people on the sidelines and grandstand care about the issue. Approaching change in this way would result in temporary solutions that could just as easily be undone. Building popular appeal, gathering feedback through checking in and reflecting on how our actions (and agitation) are moving people take time. That is one reason why using organizing tools and visuals in multiple projects can increase students' comfort level with this kind of thinking and learning.

As teachers in the classroom, we can use the field of play to track our agitational successes. At the start of the year or at the start of a unit, we can ask: Who is on the field? Who is on the sidelines? And who is in the grandstand? What teaching tactics move students on or off the field? With this in mind, we observe group work and individual behavior in the light of what is motivating and moving people. There will be the "tough to move individuals" who will be resistant to "stepping on to the field". Sometimes those are the students who hold back their participation as a form asserting one element of control in their life. This makes the times when those students do step out even more special. It's important that we, as teachers, don't get disheartened at the first "no" or the tenth. We will be ready to celebrate when the student is ready to show themselves who they can be.

Seeing Growth and Stepping onto the Field

Students step onto the field of play in all different seasons within the span of the classroom year. I remember one boy didn't particularly enjoy working with other students. He tended to be a bit shy and preferred speaking with adults. This was in part because he spent a lot of time afterschool with his grandma. In terms of schoolwork, he completed his assignments, but he kept his work to the bare minimum. That's why I noticed a change in him when it came time to learn about constructing an argument using evidence and reasoning.

Our first activity was a thumbs-up, thumbs-down exercise. I read a list of leadership attributes and asked students to give a thumbs-up if they felt the attribute was a sign of a good leader and a thumbs-down if they felt it was a sign of poor leadership. We discussed results in a one-on-one format. He was interested. Then, I dropped the clue that our study would include a trial of different leaders. He was listening. I listed out different jobs for the trial: prosecutors, defense lawyers, jurors, witnesses, a bailiff, a court reporter and a judge. He wanted to be the judge. The judge's role was to facilitate the trial, which meant calling the various participants to come to the stand, to be sworn in, to give their arguments and then respond to a few rounds of questions. It was a big job that required working with the entire class.

Dawning the black robe (that was once my graduation gown), and gripping the makeshift gavel that a student had created for me the year before, the boy was ready. "All rise!" the bailiff commanded. The court was in session. The boy executed his job with precision: summoning attorneys forward, asking for witnesses to pause while the court had time to write down key facts from their testimony—and managing the time as he wove in questions from the jury.

After the conclusion of the trial, I approached him and said, "that was fantastic. What inspired your performance?"

"Well, I watch Judge Judy with my grandma every afternoon", he said with pride. "I know what I'm doing".

He did know what he was doing, there was no question of that!

There are so many things that we try with our classes—searching for what will work. In that search, and in the daily rush that is classroom life, I have found myself thinking of people whom I share the room with, the students. Yet, in my focus on the students and what will move the students in their learning, I can forget that the grandstand extends beyond the classroom. I am reminded that we are people through other people by asking: Who are you connected to? There is a community, including grandparents who are in the grandstands, cheering on our students and supporting them from afar. Students, even reluctant ones, start to take steps forward when learning activities harmonize with out-of-school experiences. This is the power of agitation. It reveals the hidden—not in an intrusive way to the individual, but in a way that allows them to be fully them.

Agitation invites us to use the special bonds of relationship that we've forged in other places, other contexts, to take on new challenges, to step into center field and express our agency in ways that we haven't done before. We search and scratch and sift until we find the unexpected: bravery that is rooted in the mundane. Bravery that is fueled by afterschool snacks, daytime television and thousand and one expressions that is the love of our family, our community. It is the most special thing to find, because it is in each of us. When we can share it in public, it is an expansive gift that makes more people want to make their way down from the grandstand and onto the field to play, to advance the issues of our common humanity. Public bravery of this kind is true leadership.

Student in judge's robes.

"Too Soon" and the Bulldozers

In Ed Chamber's classic on organizing, *"Roots for Radicals"*, he describes a union certification drive in the South. The intent of the drive is to form a union in a workplace where there had previously been none. The organizer throws everything he has into the drive. It works—and the union gains recognition. The organizer celebrates the hard-won victory. That is, until he arrives at the factory site the next day. The factory has been locked up and word is it'll be closed for good. Not long after, a bulldozer comes and knocks the building down. The workers are devastated. The organizer turns and heads up the road to try to organize the next town. Upon his arrival, the workers and townspeople tell him to get lost. The story of the bulldozed site has traveled fast and they don't want to be seen with the organizer at all.

Reflection Questions:

Who was called into the field of play?
How did the organizer's action shift the balance of power?
What could be done to change the new balance of power?
What lessons does this story have for the teacher-as-organizer?

Organizing, like teaching, takes patience. Rushing into action can result in potential allies who are sitting in the grandstand or on the sidelines joining up with the opposition, as the story above illustrates. The more we know our people and our community, the better informed we can be in the choices that we make. It's not a stretch to imagine the application of the story of the bulldozer in the context of a classroom. The teacher-as-organizer pushes for a project to be completed, with the students just making it to the established deadline. The teacher celebrates the victory only to come into class the next day to see that the project has been destroyed. In this case, a vindictive boss isn't the source of destruction, rather a student who is frustrated with the project and/or himself and has decided that self-sabotage is better than seeing the project completed. Whether we are acting as the organizer or the teacher, we must think back to the balance of power analysis and the field of play model and ask: Are we growing capacity or undercutting capacity with our actions? I'm reminded of the saying, "There is a difference between finishing and completing a job". The organizer finished the job—ending any future actions in the immediate term of helping the workers in his area make progress. Just like the student finished his project with teacher's help—ending any future improvements by destroying his creation. In comparison, completing our jobs requires that we do the pre-action analysis that results in greater capacity for future projects, rather than a diminished sense of what can be accomplished.

That said, there are times that this lesson must be learned firsthand.

Conclusion

Learning to act takes practice. Agitation raises awareness by reaching down and reaching out. We bring new ideas to the surface when we reach down. We create new relational bonds when we reach out. Both reaching down and reaching out take energy and effort. They are antecedents to collective inquiry and collective action. To create new knowledge, we must agitate and be agitated.

This requires openness on the part of the teacher-as-organizer. Our openness to using place and time as tools of agitation is an initial step toward community connection. Using time as a tool of agitation can add varied structures that mix and match ideas and personalities within the classroom. Our reading of the classroom tells us when to "turn up" the heat or when to "dial it down". Similarly, we can view the places surrounding our schools as the staging ground for our investigations of the world. Our openness to what a place has to offer is a pathway toward student discoveries, like the backhoe that dug deep and the blue soap that became a museum.

We can also think about using tools that can be put in the hands of both teachers and students as we build classroom community strength. There is widespread benefit to our decision-making whether we apply the balance of power assessment to decisions within the classroom or within the broader school or community. We weigh trade-offs of actions and the near- and long-term effects of our actions on our ability to grow our capacity. Along these lines, the balance of power assessment asks students to think about change as a long-term project of commitment and expanding responsibility—that can be shouldered together with our partners.

Practical assessment of our capacity and the reactions to our actions can temper impulses. It can also be a helpful way to reflect following an action—did we have a realistic assessment of our own action, capacity and path for growing our capacity? Did we underestimate the response of those who might oppose our actions? Did we sell ourselves short and do too little to grow our capacity for fear of reactions? All of these help us to hone our ability to act in public in a productive manner that contributes to healthier civic spaces.

Similarly, the field of play can be used as a tool for thinking about drawing more people into public life. We know that there are many people watching the developments of the day from the grandstand, removed from the action. Issues on the field may even be only in the periphery of their view, but because we are linked by the places we share—they have the potential to influence the "game" by getting involved. This is especially true in a classroom where students are sometimes reluctant learners. They are there, but aren't totally sure if learning can be fun or "worth it". When we teach like an organizer, we have those reluctant learners in the grandstand in mind and slowly try to move them down closer to the field. We do this by consistently earning their trust and by demonstrating that our learning "actions" are fun and relevant. Trust, fun and relevance generally increase the sense that an action or a unit or a class is "worth it".

The field of play reminds us of the value in thinking of how our actions and teaching are connected to our community. Each day we have the chance to connect our learning to our students in a way that is generative—increasing the chances of more creation, imagination and connection. As teachers, starting small and using the field of play visually as a mental model for involvement can help us to move toward greater connection. It can also signal to us what is working within the class to keep students on the field, engaged and ready to push their learning objectives into "scoring position". Conversely, there may be times when things don't really go the way that we anticipated and the model again gives us the ability to visualize the shift in interest that we are observing.

Agitation is provocation. Positive stories of provocation, agitation and the deeper thinking that arise from examining the "world as it is" anew increase our capacity as educators. Sharing stories and tactics for learning gives us the courage to try something new, to stretch our imaginations—to rock the boat, maybe gently at first. From this, we get a feel for the rhythm of action and reaction. We learn to use tools like tempo, place and structure to help our students and to build community. In doing so, we start to show through our actions that "rocking the boat" or "turning up the heat" are just tools that surface what already exists in each of us—the possibility of decreasing the distance between living and learning.

Works Cited

Chambers, E. T., & Cowan, M. A. (2003). *Roots for radicals*. Continuum.

Meier, D. (1995). *The power of their ideas: Lessons for America from a small school in Harlem*. Beacon Press.

Palmer, P. J. (2017). *Courage to teach: Exploring the inner landscape of a teacher's life - 20th anniversary edition* (20th ed.). Jossey-Bass. (Original work published 1998).

Sobel, D. (2008). *Childhood and nature: Design principles for educators*. Stenhouse Publishers.

4

The Iron Rule
Forging a Path Together

When I was little, my dad and I were driving home on a snowy night. His old blue pickup truck had one wheel drive, but he had a few cinder blocks in the back bed. With his high beams on, the snow falling around us in our ascent of a winding mountain pass walled us off from the outside world. Then we lost traction. The old truck had gone about as far as it would.

We waited there on the road, on the mountain in the middle of nowhere—in northern New Hampshire.

Finally, we saw headlights. Another car approached. Pulling alongside us, they rolled down their window and asked, "Ya stuck?"

"We lost traction", my dad replied.

"Tough times. I hear ya", the driver said, rolling his window back up.

My dad turned to me and echoed the words we had just heard with a questioning tone and a north country inflection that failed to hide disbelief, "Tough times, I hear ya?"

The red taillights of the other car were ahead of us, then crested over the peak of the pass, then gone.

The Iron Rule

The Iron Rule of organizing is: *don't do for others what they can do for themselves*. This might sound harsh at first. I want to assure you that it isn't. When you apply the rule to the classroom, at first, it might make you feel like you are leaving students stranded on the side of a mountain in a snowstorm. You are not.

For students who have become accustomed to having others do for them what they can do for themselves, there may be an adjustment period where they feel like they are stranded in a snowstorm—disoriented and not knowing what to do. That, of course, is why we, the teachers, are there. We can be the driver who pulls alongside the student and offers advice and help when students are spinning their wheels. Better yet, we can offer advice and help before students start up the steep slopes of becoming independent learners. After all, we've been here before, we know the lay of the land and have a good idea of the forecast. Not only that, but we know alternative routes around treacherous terrain and we know when it's best to just pull over and rest.

The Iron Rule is already a popular idea among many in the teaching profession. Most of the time, I've found that it's popular among teachers because we want to foster a personal pride in independence. This is fine and good, but what if there are more important reasons to not do for our students what they can do for themselves? And, how do we get students to start to do a little bit for themselves when they might not have been doing too much on their own?

When we think about teaching from the perspective of an organizer, we embrace a faith in people power—that the everyday person can and should be able to effect change in their lives. This is a basic democratic principle: those closest and most impacted by the issues should have a say in how the issues are solved. In this chapter, we dig into ramp-ways for student self-directed learning as well as concepts that help us explain the rationalization for this kind of learning to our colleagues and broader educational communities, especially to those who may be reluctant to depart from tradition.

The Ladder of Engagement

Organizers think about a ladder of engagement. This is the idea that small steps over time increase the engagement of an individual or group of people by scaling up the amount of action they take. For example, an organizer thinks about asking folks at a workplace to wear a pin or the same color shirt as a "first wrung" level of engagement. It is an action that is relatively low risk. After asking everyone to wear the pin or shirt, the organizer then must see how many people took the action to judge whether it was successful. How many people participated? Is the number of people participating enough to take the next step in acting together? What is the next step?

Organizers will create an organizing committee composed of people at a worksite to build site-based leadership. Organizing committee members are leaders within the community who are organic leaders. As mentioned in previous chapters, it is the goal of the organizer to identify organic leaders—people who are already respected and recognized within the community. On

The Ladder of Engagement.

the organizing committee, the organic leaders should consider all the possible actions on the ladder of engagement that make sense for the people they work with. After brainstorming these possible actions, the committee can sort the actions from "low engagement" to "high engagement". Low engagement actions include more passive actions on the part of participants. High engagement actions would include more participatory actions. The committee may not end up using all the actions that they brainstorm and sort. They want to think widely and then hone in on the actions that make the most sense for their particular situation.

Teacher Committee Sorting Example

Imagine being on an organizing committee at your school. Place the following items on the Ladder of Engagement: sign a petition, create pins, wear pins, write a speech to be given at the school board, show up at a 5-minute meeting where you gather together 10–15 members of your staff, attend a school board meeting, hold signs at a polling station and stamp postcards that can be sent out prior to a contract vote.

(adapted from *Secrets of a Successful Organizer*)

The ladder of engagement is directly transferable to the classroom. As teachers, we can use the ladder of engagement to imagine the different activities that our classes might do in a unit. Sorting those activities along the continuum of engagement can help us to build toward lessons that require more active participation. We don't have to use all the ideas that we have, but it can help us to track how we feel students are engaging in material and how we might mix things up according to our observations.

Unit Planning for Engagement: Design and Launch

Imagine you are planning out a unit. Place the following items on the ladder of engagement:

Reading aloud (as the teacher) a passage to the class, students ranking the persuasiveness of claims about a topic from 1–5, students competing in a timed brainstorm, students sketching design ideas for a product to solve a problem, students developing product pitches, students delivering product pitches to an audience of their peers, students acting as judges for peer made products, students creating playlists and DJing as products are pitched, students holding a mock press conference about an issue related to their product, students creating product names and students testing products with users and gathering feedback.

Engagement is one aspect of how we can plan in a manner that accounts for the "Iron rule". If we are determined to not do for students what they can do for themselves, then we need to nurture their engagement. In this regard, engagement involves a sense of heightened involvement in the activity at hand. It's the feeling that our actions and participation matter—a sense of agency driven by high salience. This contrasts with the idea of engagement as a relentless attention pulling magnet. The engineered magnetism of social media is a shallow form of engagement meant to monetize our attention for the economic gain of companies. Despite its shallowness, monetized attentional engagement, is ubiquitous and corrosive. It eats away at civic life. While we cannot ignore its presence or affect, we can draw attention to how relational and place-based engagement hold promise for adding depth in the classroom setting. This starts with visualizing engagement in our classrooms and expands as we imagine ways we can work alongside our students to increase their interest in the learning and their relationship to the learning.

The Mountain of Agency (The Big Unit View)

> "Out of a mountain of despair, a stone of hope"
> —MLK

Starting a new unit can feel like an overwhelming challenge from the teacher's perspective. It can also be a time of excitement. The tension between the feelings of anxiety of excitement is the force of creativity. We can seize these moments when we are aware of how our feelings are alerting us. Sensing anxiety in our bodies and choosing to take the next step are an assertion of our creativity—and when we learn how to take those steps as teachers, we can then learn how to help students take steps into living a purpose filled life of agency.

Learning to take the first step is something that we must do. No one else can do it for us. We cannot take the first step away from anxiety for our students. They must do it. Others can be there for us, if we need it, just as we can be there for our students, if they need it. Others can help us to reflect once we have taken the step, if we need it, just as we can reflect with our students if they need it. And others can help us to plan the next step(s), if we need it, just as we can help our students to plan their next step(s), if they need it. At every point—we are grounded in respect for the relationship between ourselves and our growing capacity, just as we are grounded in respect for the relationship between our students and their growing capacity. This respect is shown through our presence, our modeling and our listening.

Our confidence and resolve may be strengthened through knowledge of similar journeys that others have taken. We are fortunate that there are many people in our lives who have found the courage to take steps out of anxiety and into the creative life, remaining curious along the way. Some of these teachings appear in Chapter 5 where we discuss the growth of community connections. Here, I would like to introduce the visual of the mountain climb as a model for the journey toward greater agency in our lives and in the classroom.

The visual of the "mountain of agency" is one way to start to think about our work of creating classroom community space where students can achieve their goals. The big goal for the unit can be called the "mountain top" goal. Some schools, like my own, use language like "formative assessment" and "summative assessment", which I think fits well with the mountain model. For those unfamiliar with these terms, a "formative assessment" is the small assignments or check-ins that we, as teachers, can use during the unit to make sure that student learning is on the right path. As I say to my students, the "summative assessment" is like the summit of the learning—it's the top and final chance in the unit to show the progress that you've made in your learning. By the end of each unit, students demonstrate their agency in applying different skills or knowledge.

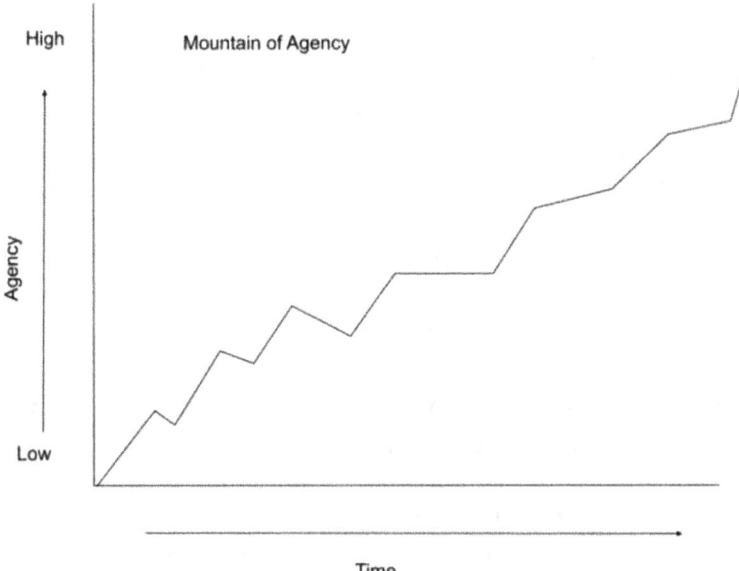

Mountain of Agency.

In the world of organizing, this model has been used for things like contract campaigns. Organizing committees decide together what they would like to set as their "mountain top" goal. The goal can be straightforward like: win a fair contract or win a fair contract where members gain a 6% raise. The goal can be written at the top right of the chart and posted in a place where everyone can see it and be reminded of the mission of our immediate work together. From that point, the organizing committee can map out the actions that can move the group toward accomplishing the goal.

Similarly, from the point of view of the teacher, the mountain model can help us in planning out a unit. Many in the profession refer to the general concept of setting the goal for a unit and mapping out the intermediate learning activities as "planning backward" or "understanding by design" (UBD) (Wiggins & McTighe, 2005). I think the advantage of the mountain model over some of the understanding by design templates that I've encountered over the years is its accessibility. The mountain as metaphor reinforces the process of planning, plateauing, evaluating and adjusting. Each activity that we plan becomes a point of inflection along the journey to the top of the summit. For students, this explanation increases the predictability of the class and opens up the black-box that can be planning, at least a little bit. Again, this is a possible ramp-way to supporting further student agency.

The mountain model can also be used as a reflection tool for classes that are looking to take another step toward increasing student agency. Teachers identify the goal for the unit and keep that goal visible (some like to post it on a bulletin board). Periodically, we can ask our classes to add to the bulletin board through prompts and questions like:

- Summarize today's lesson
- What was one thing from today that helped you to move closer to the mountain top?
- What is one question that you have from today's class?
- What next step do you want to take in your project/learning?

These short end-of-class questions are popularly referred to as "exit tickets". Asking for a few volunteers to share out responses and keeping a visual record of the responses help students to reflect on their work and to think about how their learning is connected to the "big picture". It can also help to build anticipation for future learning.

Student exposure to the mountain model also allows for the transfer of planning from teacher to student. Students who have gained familiarity with the model through their teacher talking about the small steps and activities that help us to climb to the summit can then start to identify their own small stops (or small goals) that can help them to reach larger learning goals. This concept isn't new as Rogers (1969) wrote about teachers using a learning model where the teacher identified the larger learning goal while providing students with latitude for demonstrating their ability to meet the goal. Rogers' suggestions came from a desire to foster agency and intellectual curiosity while operating within the established school system.

The class leader speaks to the group about the next goals that we should pursue.

In this respect, for teachers looking to accelerate student agency, the mountain model can be a useful outline for generating plans and conversation among students. Supplemental questions that could support these conversation include:

- What is the learning goal?
- What could students create to demonstrate the goal?
- What are three to five jobs that contribute to the creation?
- What jobs need to be prioritized and what is the timeline for creation given the due date for the final product? (place those jobs in order on the peaks)
- What adjustments need to be made? (ongoing assessment)

Students can create a mountain model as a team using these questions. Each group within the class can then present their model to the class and receive both informal and formal feedback. The informal feedback can be in the form of observations the students make about other's presentations. What did other groups share that could help strengthen the proposal/strategy? The formal feedback can be in the form of sticky notes—where each group provides simple suggestions on sticky notes on one specific element of the shared proposal that was well done and one specific thing that could help the group make the next step in their learning.

Planning, prioritizing and sequencing our learning actions over time is a practice of creating a strategy for achieving our "mountain top" goal. There are many paths to the mountain top and we need to pick the one that best matches what we need as teachers and what our students need. We can introduce the concept of the mountain top goal for a unit. We can introduce the goal and chart the intermediate activities that we do together. We can use the mountain model as a reflection tool. We can provide the big goal and use the mountain model as a way for students to plan their own learning and to provide feedback to one another. The flexibility and accessibility of the model allows us as teachers to find what works best for our circumstances. We know that our circumstances can change, which means having a flexible model that can change supports the adaptive nature of our work.

Applying AEIOU to Plastic

Gathering: Tuning in and Being Agitated by What We Accumulate

In this section, I will discuss how to use elements of the AEIOU organizing framework to create a unit. As I teach and plan, the framework is a guiding reference point. As such, it's not determinative. It helps give me a point of orientation. I'll return to parts of the framework as needed as the unit progresses. We agitate if we need more agitation to help us gain more momentum for a phase of the learning. The same can be said in terms of applying any other aspect of AEIOU. I have found that the flexibility of the framework creates breathing room to practice The Iron Rule: don't do for others what they can do for themselves. The trajectory of student agency within our classroom necessitates that there be space for both the predictability of routine and adaptations based on student interest and ability. It's all about taking what we have to get what we need so that we can achieve what we want. In this case, I had a classroom of sixth graders and the tricky issue of plastic bags that keep overflowing at our homes.

I cannot help but to accumulate papers on my desk at school. These are the papers that I need to grade, papers that I set aside in hopes of reusing as scrap and the papers that sit waiting to be used for future lessons. It's easy to collect things.

One of the lessons that I've learned as I've tried to practice teaching as an organizer is to pay attention to what I'm collecting, what is accumulating. Sometimes we have to be surrounded by a pile of what we have collected before we realize that we have to do something about it.

I find that this is the case with single-use plastic bags. Despite using reusable bags for groceries, a collection of plastic bags grows and overflows by my sink. The conspicuous presence of plastic bags at home and out in the world agitated my curiosity. There must be a lesson here,

I thought to myself. Still, I wasn't sure what the lesson was exactly—and I decided to figure it out with my students, knowing that I had the broader geographic theme of "human environmental interaction" to weave into the curriculum.

With time for starting a new unit ticking down, I asked students to bring in any spare plastic bags at home. Of course, everyone has their own stockpile of these vestiges of consumption and convenience. Most families were more than happy to see their bags leave home—no questions asked.

Each day at the start of class, I would ask students if they had brought in any plastic bags. Students started dropping off bags in the morning when they arrived at school and in between classes during our "transition time". I let the pile grow in the front of the classroom...and grow...and grow. Students would ask and ask and ask what the deal with bags was. What are we going to do with them? Is there something we can do with them? I let these questions accumulate, just like the pile of bags, as we finished one unit and prepared to start a new one using the bags as the primary provocation and issue.

Returning to Sobel's principles, I used the design principle of "animal allies" to heighten student interest at the start of our new inquiry. "What animals do you think are most affected by plastic bags?" I asked the class. Small groups brainstormed lists of animals and then we built a whole class list. "This is a pretty good list" I said, "But what categories could we group all these animals into?" We listened to a few different ideas for groupings before circling the names of animals on the board into clusters and labeling them according to what appeared to be the class consensus. Groupings often arranged along the lines of: birds, customers, turtles, whales, various fish, and fishermen. "Humans are animals", students like to remind one another in this exercise. I'm not sure if Sobel had humans in mind when he was imagining his design principles, but I think that it works well for the kind of perspective exploring that we do in class.

At this point, we're ready to move into the "educate" phase of AEIOU. This is where we'll start to explore perspectives and dig a little deeper into the facts surrounding the issue of plastic bags. I ask students to pick one group and one animal from that group. I'll do a quick check-in to make sure we have a wide variety of perspectives in the groups, asking for a few volunteers to switch if we are a little too lopsided. With a balance of perspectives, it's time to introduce the "Exploring Perspectives" diagram "(see on following page).

"Exploring Perspectives" or as some students refer to the diagram, "the circle guy", is a way for students to start to think about an issue from a single perspective. If it's the first time that students have seen this diagram, I'll draw a big version of it on the board and give an example of how we can approach this style of thinking. This kind of activity can be a helpful pre-reading tool. It activates students' prior knowledge on the topic and asks them to anticipate what they might find out if given time to dig into the facts. Initially, students will write down dot point answers, which don't need to be complete sentences for each of the following questions that go with the diagram (you can substitute any issue in for where I've added plastic):

Exploring senses:

Where does ____ see plastic? What does s/he see?

What does _____ think about plastic? (interpret what s/he sees)

What does _____ hear from other animals about plastic? What does s/he hear when near plastic?

What does plastic feel like when s/he touches it?

Exploring opinions

What does s/he say about plastic when talking with friends/family?

Going inside

How does plastic affect those s/he loves? How does it affect the place(s) s/he loves?

What fears does s/he have about plastic?

What kind of future does s/he want with plastic?

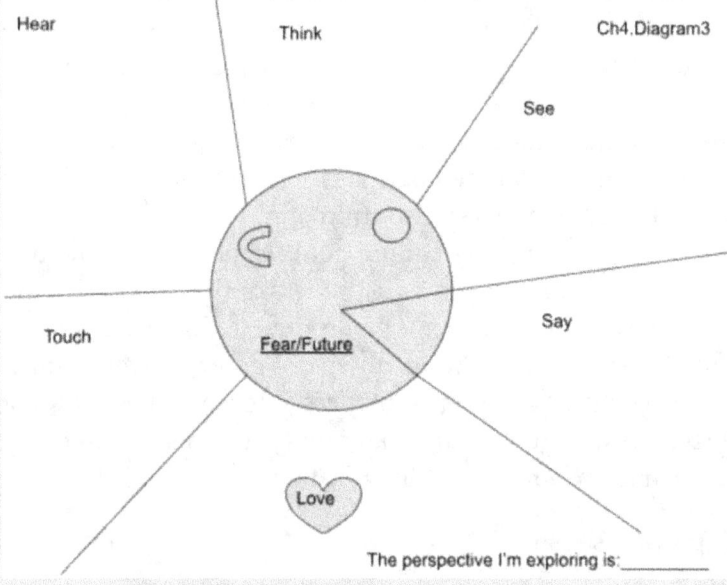

Exploring Perspectives.

    Perspective taking can be a real challenge at the middle school level, which is why I encourage students to share what they come up with from this activity with one another. Oftentimes, hearing how others have approached this open-ended work can give students the confidence needed to try out new ideas and do a little more digging into the perspective that they are exploring. Finding the gossipy guppy fish who wants to dish on how plastic has been affecting their "school" can help lighten the mood. There will be time for more seriousness later and a mix of perspectives can uplift creativity rather than shutting down discussion with pure gloom—though we all develop our own sense of this balance, especially depending on the topic that we're studying.

It's time to start into the research phase of the unit following our initial foray into the thoughts and hearts of the animals. Anticipating some of the potential categories of student interest can help with the prep work that is needed to support the next step of the learning: digging into the research. I try to gather a collection of digital resources that include videos, articles of varied lengths and complexities, diagrams, charts and infographics that can get students started on their research. Each group will have a set of these resources that go along with their perspective (for example, those interested in birds will have resources specifically about how birds are affected by plastic). Once students have started to look at the resources, I'll add more to the collections based on their interests (what they want to know more about) and their suggestions (students are always finding sources). I always have more than enough resources for students to complete the research phase without journeying into the wider web of online searching. There are, of course, a number of opinions about whether to allow students to search the web on their own or if it's suitable to have them use only pre-curated resources. My suggestion is to simply do what works best for you and your students. Discussions around the credibility of resources that students find can be a valuable lesson in itself, yet not something that I'll delve into here.

Typically, I ask students to look for facts that can tell the story of how their chosen animal is being affected by plastic. For this, I look for students to provide factual evidence that they can explain and cite. For example, some students might write about how the percentage of seabirds with plastic inside of them has increased from 5% in 1960 to 90% in 2015 (Levey, 2015). They would then go on to explain what this meant for the seabirds—perhaps describing how there are now more birds observed to have died from ingesting plastic. This plastic problem, students might argue, is a direct threat to humans as birds can be an indicator species that point to greater ecological strain that can affect humans. Students could go further with their explanation and eventually wrap up with noting the author and the year of publication: Levey (2015).

I ask students to look into possible solutions to the issue through their research as well. This has led students to find out about countries, states, cities and towns that have banned plastic bags. It has led to students to investigate taxing the use of plastic bags. It has led to students looking into ways to encourage shoppers to buy reusable bags. And it has brought students to find out about efforts to repurpose plastic bags. All of these solutions and more are brought to the table as we continue to educate ourselves on the issues and solutions that have been tried in the world.

At this point in our unit progression, I'll show a few videos of press conferences featuring known athletes. I'll show LeBron James and Caitlin Clark fielding questions, adjusting the athletes depending on the sport preferences of the class. But the key is to start to imagine what it's like to speak about your experiences, share your knowledge and be in the "limelight" of a press conference. This is my basic way to assuage fears students might have for our own mini-press conference on plastic. Student worries about speaking usually decrease when they find they can work with their groupmates to craft prepared remarks and that they can work together to respond to any tough questions that they may get from the "reporters" (a press pool of students from other groups).

Students work together, reflecting on their researched notes, to create prepared statements on the issues facing their group of animals. I encourage students to use their creative writing from "exploring perspectives" as a framing for facts that tell the story of how the animals are affected by plastic. I also provide an optional template to help students get started. For the template, I have sentence stems that connect back to "exploring perspectives":

> I'm here on behalf of the _____ (seagulls, turtles, etc.) today to tell you about the issues that we face regarding plastic pollution
>
> Each day, I see... _____ (use your research notes to provide facts and explanation of what they see).
>
> I feel that one thing that there is currently a lack of understanding about plastic is... _____ (explain what folks need to know and why they need to know it).
>
> I want you to consider _____ as a possible solution (provide reasoning).
>
> Finally, in closing today, a question that I would like you all to consider is...._____.

This kind of framing supports students in assimilating their background knowledge with their researched evidence. The result is often a compelling statement on behalf of the animals that challenges assumptions and pushes the boundaries of discussion around the effect of plastic pollution as symbolized and embodied by our mound of plastic bags that sits in the front of the classroom.

The plastic bags start to take shape here—and not just in the sense that we become aware of their impact on the environment. I slowly start to gather the bags, making bags filled with bags. The shape is undecipherable at first, but then I pull out an old school jacket that I keep stashed in my teacher's closet. I stuff a bag with even more bags into the jacket, filling out the torso and then the limbs—a plastic bag scarecrow takes shape. The jacket has a hood, which is the perfect place to pack in more bags that become the head. The blank bag face is always met by the markers of a student who can't resist the crinkly canvas. Agitation drives participation and the co-creation of the villainous "plastic bag man" becomes the symbol of our frustration with single-use plastic.

Students help to rearrange the room before we set up for the plastic bag press conference. We place a long rectangular table in the front of the room. A student occasionally prepares a slide background that can be projected behind the table with an image of a plastic bag and headlines like: "Official Presser of the Plastic Bag" or "Plastic Bag News". These images help to set the tone of the press conference, similar to the sleek custom media backdrops of the National Basketball Association (NBA) or Cable News Network (CNN). Students also enjoy picking out a short clip of intro theme music for the press conference, something that focuses attention and signals to the audience that official business is about to begin. My personal preference is the theme song of the longrunning political show, "Meet the Press", but I take recommendations from the class and seek a student to be our "DJ" for the event. All of these small actions that help prepare us for the press conference are invitations to do the "job distribution" part of organizing—sorting out interests and finding who would like to make their own little contribution from the creation of plastic bag man (students will bring in their own outfits for him), to the set design, to the music—all small ways that can invite personalization, flare and enjoyment. It might seem trivial, but when organizing is fun it starts a virtuous cycle of participation that helps us reach for new heights on "Agency Mountain".

We decide on an order for each group to present just before it's time to begin the press conference. I'll mock up a little script for a student correspondent who would like to serve as the host. In the script, the host will welcome the press to the presser and review the operating procedure. The team sitting at the front table will provide their statement, which can include each member of the team sharing their own prepared remarks, followed by their prepared question to the pool of reporters. After the prepared remarks, the members of the press (the rest of the class who aren't at the podium as part of the presenting team) can raise their hand to be acknowledged by the host and to ask a question. The member of the press corps who is asking the question should stand upon being acknowledged and state their credentials before asking their question. For example, a reporter who has been called on who has researched the effect of plastic on turtles may stand and say, "My name is Jill and I'm with "The Turtle Times. My question is, 'could you speak to how plastic pollution has affected your home?'" The team at the podium can take a moment to talk among themselves and look at their notes before responding with their most fact-based answer. Typically, the host is asked to keep track of time, try to involve as many perspectives and reporters as possible and to keep the question session to 5–7 minutes total. At the conclusion of the question and answer session, the host will cue the disk jockey (DJ) to play the theme music, which signals a transition of the teams. The next team will come forward to be introduced by the host and the process will repeat itself.

I ask students to take notes on questions asked and responses given as the press conference is happening. To do this, I'll create a paper that has two columns. One column will be for questions asked and the other for responses. Students know that our goal is to gather more evidence that can help us to see the issue from multiple viewpoints. It's not necessary to write down everything, but it is necessary to try and discern what is important. That is the challenging part of participating in a group discussion—and developing one's discernment means listening, adding more to your collective knowledge on a topic and sorting through what you've found out based on your expanded understanding of the given topic. For this reason, I try to give several chances for students to show that they're refining their understanding over the course of a unit.

It can take two days for all the groups to present their prepared remarks at the podium, to ask questions and to respond. Once we are ready to move on, the class moves toward a summary of what they've learned so far. This has taken different forms over the years. At times, students will produce a short video news report or a brief newspaper article representing their team's viewpoint. Other times, students will write a one paragraph brief addressing a question that was asked during the presser that they thought was important.

From Problems to Issues

One thing that we hear from the press conference proceedings is that the problem of plastic pollution is so big. Even though we started small with the plastic bags that were taking up space at our homes—we quickly came to see that nearly every animal seems to be touched by plastic in one form or another. I don't like to leave students feeling stranded with problems that are too big to act on—so I try to shrink the problem down to a level that we interact with every day. This isn't to say that larger policy solutions aren't important, of course they are. My decision, as a teacher, is to try to remain with my feet firmly in the world as it is, inviting students to imagine the world as it could be, using place and our principles to narrow the gap between "is" and "ought to".

Students have been eyeing "plastic bag man" with curiosity and feigned contempt—and they are ready to create a solution in the culminating stage of our unit. "We've learned about how animals are affected by plastic pollution–we've seen bags and other single-use plastic pile up at our homes", I say to the class before posing the big question, "now what are we going to do about it?"

It's time for a final bit of provocation. I switch to my other role as CEO of Goodwin Worldwide Inc., where I wear a wrinkled black pinstriped suit jacket and put on my "infomercial" voice. "Ladies and gentlemen, it's come to my attention that there was recently a press conference where my company's wonderful world famous product, plastic bags, were discussed." At this point, a student will often interrupt and makes a comment like, "you're ruining the Earth!" Pausing, I invite the ire of students that to this point has been reserved for the "plastic bag man". Then, I continue, "In light of this bad press, Goodwin Worldwide Inc. has decided to go green. I mean, for us, it's always been about the green. If you think about it–our pursuit of those green dollar, dollar bills has always guided us..." I trail off as if being caught up in my own daydream about dollars. I snap back to reality to finish my pitch, "That's where all you folks come in: we need your ideas for new products. The catch, you ask? There is no catch...just that you can only use recycled materials (things that would otherwise be thrown away or recycled) to create the best possible upcycled product".

To expand our vision of the type of products that we might make, we watch a couple of short videos that use plastic bags for art installations. *The Plastic Bag Store* is a fan favorite of an installation with various iterations including in Australia (2021), at the University of North Carolina-Chapel Hill (2018) and with the Massachusetts Museum of Contemporary Art (MassMoCo, 2024). *The Plastic Bag Store* imagines a grocery store where everything is made of plastic and all the names of products are edgy and related to plastic pollution. From there, I turn it over to the students to start to plan their own products as teams.

This is a stage of thinking where we want a free flow of ideas and for students to express their interests. While developing a plan as a group, I ask that the teams of students consider the following questions and prompts:

- ◆ Audience: Who would use or interact or view your product?
- ◆ Materials: What materials do you have that are readily available at home? Who will bring in what?

- Name: What is your product's name?
- Pitch: What is a short pitch that highlights your product, its features and its green appeal?
- Design: Sketch a rough diagram of your product.

Many students know exactly what they want to create. Still, others need a little more support. For those who need that extra support, I supply examples of written pitches, product names and explanations of each. Students also have access to a slideshow that features photos from past projects, photos of product ideas from the wider web and how-to videos for creating some products. One children's book that I've found to also be inspiring for some students is *One Plastic Bag* (Paul & Zunon, 2017), which tells the story of Isatou Ceesay, a Gambian environmentalist who turned plastic bags into beautiful purses. All these resources are an option for students—and give them a chance to decide for themselves what fits their needs in this work.

Another helpful tool that can assist students who need some extra support is the "Who/Do" list. This is a two-column chart where you list out the jobs that need to get done on the team and who is going to do each of the jobs. The "Who/Do" is an easy way to help facilitate job delegation, which is the "O" for "organizing" in the AEIOU framework. Keeping a running list of tasks and who the group members are who are completing those tasks helps students to track new needs for the group work as the project develops.

I circulate around the room and help teams troubleshoot their prototypes as students work over the next week. There are design attempts that end up crumpled up or discarded each day—trial balloons that simply don't take. I ask questions to try to move the teams toward considering how the user of the product may be affected or interact with the design. It can be common for students to want to make something for themselves, which is fine, but I try to push their thinking about the purpose of their work with questions like:

- Who is this designed for?
- How will they use it or interact with it?

- What do you want the user or view to feel?
- What's the next step to moving forward to improving its use or feel?

These questions relate back to the principle of putting people first. If we are creating something for ourselves, we want to make sure that what we create is meeting our needs. If we are creating a product for someone else, we want to consider how they might use it and how we make it as useful for this purpose as possible. And if we are working on a project for public viewing, we want to consider the feelings that our work evokes in our viewers—maybe there is a way we can enhance the feeling(s) that we seek to evoke. Putting people first in our work is not meant to be commercial, though these skills can have commercial uses. Instead it's meant to prioritize our purposeful use of what we have as we seek connection with others in our community.

It then becomes an open invitation to students to think about repurposing or upcycling the bags. Students have come up with all kinds of creative ideas in the past, ideas that keep the bags out of local landfills. One student went on to work with a community church and expanded her idea to creating plarn (plastic yarn) out of the bags. She then wove mats that people experiencing homelessness could use to stay off the ground. Others have used weaving similar to the type modeled by Isatou Ceesay's story and created durable bags out of plastic.

Similar to asking questions to clarify the people-first purpose of our work, in the pitch part of the project students explained their work to engage the audience purposefully. In creating pitches for their products, students use elements of public narrative. They identify a problem (related to plastic), the choice that the audience or potential user can make and the outcome of taking action. One team member often takes on the job of working on developing a pitch. Many prefer to record their pitches using a video tool, which allows the creator to record, view and critique their own work. This isn't a substitute for talking with people in person, but a way to practice gaining increased confidence in honing and delivering a short narrative.

Slowly, as we start to see designs take shape, I try another attempt at organizing the teams. I invite teams to write their ideas for products on the board. From that list, I ask students if there are any uniting themes that they see among the product ideas that we could use as a forum for sharing our work. For example, the grocery store from *"The Plastic Bag Store"* art exhibit uses the store setting as a public facing stage for performance. There are classes that settle on a theme that works for everyone and there are times when teams want to try a format for sharing that is a little more traditional (speaking to the class in a lecture kind of format). My goal is to facilitate a conversation with the students about what they think will work for them and their products. I'll record the options that the class was thinking about if we don't settle on an idea right away and we can let it simmer for a few days until the group is ready to make their decision. This simmering strategy can allow students to talk with peers from other classes and exchange ideas with students outside their own class period.

In our most recent rendition of this project, each class decided to go with a run-way fashion show as the culminating event. Not every group had wearable products, but that didn't stop them from finding ways to strike a pose with the product and to demonstrate its use. Again, we sought to have a DJ, and one student suggested we use the music from the TV show "Dress to Impress" to provide the right ambiance(In full disclosure, this is a show that I still have not seen). The theme song had the sound of paparazzi cameras clicking and flashing to a steady base beat. Since the show was all about upcycling, we unfolded cardboard boxes to form a "recycled runway" or a "cardboard carpet" that started at the classroom door, turned in the middle of the room to head toward the front of the room and then spanned most of the width of the front of the classroom. Again, students volunteered to host the event, compiling an order for those who would walk the "cardboard carpet" and short descriptions of their wares.

Classes asked that the top two or three finishers from each period advance to a teamwide run-way challenge. This would mean about ten teams sharing their work to the other 70 or so students. To aid in the difficult task, student judges created a scoring rubric that included categories like: "creative use of materials" and "usefulness in the real world". The competition aspect of the upcycle fashion show further encouraged teams to share their flare on the "cardboard carpet". There was a generally supportive atmosphere with the different teams influencing one another's presentation styles and each group openly cheering on the next "competitor". Hosts artfully introduced each team in coordination with the DJ. The judges would announce their scores following the completion of each "cardboard carpet" routine.

The top placing design for 2025 was a wedding party, replete with a wedding gown with a long plastic bag train and plastic flowers. Other top finishers included a team that made an athletic shoe with a styrofoam sole, and a team with a trash-bag layered dress. Each of the top groups showed their creations on the runway in front of the large group of their peers. The wedding group paused before taking the stage, nodding to the DJ, the music changed to "here comes the bride". Their processional started with a slow march up the aisle, where a group member who was donning a drooping cardboard mustache moved to center stage to serve as the officiant. The crowd went silent before breaking into cheers at the conclusion of the short ceremony. A bouquet of plastic flowers was thrown and the processional exited the runway—an uplifting champion of our upcycle challenge.

Upcycle Conclusion

Teaching like an organizer is easier when you use the AEIOU framework and remain open to its iterative nature, which is responsive to student needs. I often find dialogue between the students to be a core element of the "education" step of the framework. Students teaching one another what they have learned is a rich experience and underlies the kind of continuous relationship building that is at the core of organizing. Rather than directing attention to the adult as the disseminator of knowledge—they come to see themselves and their peers as active creators of knowledge and power. This isn't to say that direct instruction has no place. It has a time and use. Acting together requires that we learn to see one another as the unique sources of strength and creativity that we are.

The use of "agitation" gives the teacher a tool to resurface the tensions within the issue. "Agitation" helps us to build a dramatic arc for our classroom activities. It can serve as motivation for participation and a guide back to our purpose for acting. Our questions nudge and probe student thinking, not in an attempt to overtake the act of creation, but to test the underlying ideas and assumptions in a manner that is clarifying for the students.

Keeping "innoculation" in mind grants the teacher a tool of reassurance. We point to the little bit of the big thing that the student has done as a proof point for what they can accomplish, despite their fears or anxiety. Your small successes are indicators of what you can do. This is not denying that fear exists or that fear is real to the student. It's acknowledging the fear and working with the student to find their path through it.

"Organizing" keeps us thinking about how we are inviting students into the decision-making process. Each small way that we involve them, check-in with them and attempt to weave their voices into the ongoing classroom work creates an opportunity for a transfer of responsibility of learning to the learners. There is a wide range of how this can look in the classroom—and the most important part is that we keep looking for those places where we feel like the students are ready to engage. This is especially true in the traditional public school setting—where there are many mandates and where every small step we take as teachers to create a more progressive classroom is a chance to keep moving forward for our students who might be less familiar with having a role in shaping their learning.

Celebrating how far we have come as teachers and as a class keeps us going. We uplift ourselves as teachers when we are patient in our own development. This can be difficult since we have to be ready for the thousands of decisions that we make every single day. At the same time, when we see just how much we're doing, just how worn down we can get, there is a great chance for each of us to practice patience.

I think that patience is especially difficult to practice when you feel like you're trying to just make it to the next day—just trying to survive. It can feel like patience is extending our view up from surviving the next day to instead looking to the horizon of the week or month, or whatever increment allows us to slow the pace for ourselves. This may make sense for some.

Another way we can shift our perspective on patience is to look at what we have done. We uplift the work that we have done. We say to ourselves, it took persistence on our part to make it this far and practicing patience is how we honor and sustain that persistence into the future. In recognizing our own strength, we become strong.

Our strength as teachers allows us to find authentic ways to uplift our students. We can only uplift when we are known by our students and know our students. There are many suggestions in the world of teaching about celebrating learning—and we can draw on them as inspiration, but the most important thing is that we find ways that celebrate and uplift that are meaningful to our students as learners and people. Oftentimes, students have ideas about what would be a meaningful way for their learning and achievements to be celebrated. From the viewpoint of the teacher, asking permission is important to uplifting—"would you be interested in…" and "would it be okay if we tried…" are phrases that I find myself using to see if students are okay with sharing their work or ideas with others. These simple asks show respect to the students and reinforce their importance to our learning community. I had never thought of uplifting student learning and agency through a fashion show, nevertheless, we did. I had never imagined that we could uplift student work through creating space for a wedding crafted out of recycled materials, nevertheless, we did. A virtuous cycle is created in the classroom through our openness to listening, seeking permission, recognizing, persisting and uplifting. It is through patiently following this spiraling cycle that we invite our classes to pursue change, both in themselves and in their community.

Reflecting and Extending: Create a mountain model for the unit described above. Plot out the learning activities that we completed. Consider the class's use of elements of the AEIOU framework. Label each activity that you identify as AEIO or U. Look at a unit that you have created in the past. Can you identify aspects of AEIOU in it? Are there elements that you would now add?

Workers' Lives on the Line

What Are the Hidden Costs of Our Shirts?

My first encounter with the word agitation was on the dial of our washing machine growing up. It had something to do with getting the mud off my pants, I figured. It was around this time that I started asking my mom to cut the tags off my t-shirts and pants. They were too itchy, I said.

Years later, as a teacher, my thoughts returned to these tags. They had something to say too. Their tiny print said things like, "machine wash" "Tumble dry" and "made in Vietnam". These words held meaning. These words could agitate. And while I had asked to have the tags cut off my own clothing as a kid, I wondered how we might better understand our connection to the clothing that we wear each day by following the agitational mantra of "making the invisible, visible" as a class.

This year, working with sixth graders, I framed our unit on globalization with the question: What are the hidden costs of our shirts?

There is so much that can remain invisible: entire lives, countries, generations of upheaval and struggle. The unseen surrounds us and calls us to learn more, to become engaged and to weigh our personal and collective decisions.

Our class starts with looking at the tags on our own shirts. "What country do you think is the most common manufacturer in our classroom?" I ask. "China", students reliably answer. Yet, every year the results change, as fashion changes and as the global economy changes.

What doesn't change is the demand for more shirts. Our school buys hundreds of t-shirts every year. Families pay ten dollars. "Ah, the cost isn't hidden, Mr. Goodwin. It's ten bucks", a student named Ben says.

But is what you spend the only cost?

Viewing a short video produced by NPR's *Planet Money*, our class learns about the life of one worker in the Bangladeshi garment business, Jasmine. Still a teen,

Jasmine has traveled over six hours away from her family and hometown to find a job. She explains that her sister had been married off at a similar age, and her family was forced into debt to pay for her dowry.

Near the factory in Dhaka, Jasmine has a small room—all her belongings fit on one shelf. There is no running water or indoor plumbing. She saves money to send home and slowly helps her family out of debt.

The infamous disaster at Rana Plaza in (2012) demonstrates the awful risks that workers like Jasmine take to escape poverty and the bondage of patriarchal tradition. She and her fellow workers risk personal safety and well-being to earn among the lowest wages in the world.

As new tariffs are imposed on places like Vietnam and Bangladesh, the places that have been the cutting room floors of the world's lust for fast fashion, it is the lives of people like Jasmine that will likely be further disrupted, the most vulnerable left to carry the heaviest of burdens once again.

The Past is Now

"But Bangladesh is far away. The lack of safety in the factories, the low pay, the desperate living conditions…it couldn't happen here, right?" is a question that reverberates in class. It's a question that searches for both reassurance and for a sign of progress. It's a question that is sometimes thought or said quietly but not to the whole group because it has a hardness to it. Yet, given the chance to breathe, the question also opens itself to telling a story of everyday people taking action, of workers forming a line of solidarity to improve the lives of one another.

The grainy photographs of Jacob Riis (1890), further weathered by my finicky copy machine, tell us the story. We do a "museum walk" around the room, interpreting and analyzing these images of a time when child labor laws were loose, if existent at all. Posted on the classroom walls, photos of the dark bags under the eyes of child laborers tell us, "It started here…don't look away".

I pause with Cal, who is looking at a photo titled, "five cents a spot". It shows a crowded room, there's a kind of makeshift bunk bed, weary workers lifting their heads above a mess of blankets, a satchel hangs from the wall. "It's like an echo," she whispers.

Another group of students has found a photo of women raising a banner for the "Ladies Waist and Dressmakers Union".

"Why are they all women?" Izzy asks before continuing to add, "Why has it been mostly women in the videos and pictures of people making shirts today?"

All of these questions are gathered on a simple "See, Think, Wonder" graphic organizer. They're a collection of interpretations that we can refer to as students think more critically about our role in this complex history and global network of trade.

In the next lesson, we come back to our questions. Thinking about what we've seen and have been learning about so far, while keeping our central question in mind, we use the "Right Question" protocol to brainstorm possible supporting research questions (The Right Question Institute, 2018). The guidelines of the protocol are simple: work as a team, during the established amount of time keep asking questions, it may be tempting to answer questions—so anytime you hear someone making a statement turn it into a question and write down all questions (all questions are good questions).

Creating the Line

We number our questions after five minutes of brainstorming and teams discuss what they feel their top three questions are. Each team will then send a representative to the white board in the front of the class to share and write down their questions. Hearing the questions from other teams of students sometimes will generate new questions, and that's fine. Groups select one question from the many we brainstorm to use as a central question for inquiry.

Using the articles, photographs and videos that we've reviewed, students create visual artifacts of their own that help to answer their group's selected question. The sixth graders create poetry, draw images, create their own sketches of t-shirts with messages on them and type up descriptions and short analysis meant to help their audience think more deeply about their research.

One group picked the question, "What would it be like to survive on so little money?" A boy drew a bookshelf imagining the few items that workers might own. His partner in the group wrote a poem describing all the things workers must use their limited earnings on just to survive—and what is left—no option but to head back to work to restart the cycle of survival.

Another group sketched a LeBron James jersey. They decided to compare LeBron's wages, which they calculated per minute to the monthly wages earned by the workers in Bangladesh that produce his apparel. Their bar graph shows a towering yellow bar representing LeBron's minute of earnings and a small green sliver that you must look closely at to even tell that it represents the meager earnings of the shirt makers. This chart gets peers questioning: How could one person make so much money in a minute while another person doesn't come close to that in a whole month? The economic reality hits hard.

Still, a girl in a neighboring group, inspired by the photos she had seen of the immigrant women hitting the street in New York to redefine labor, designed a logo for a women's garment union, drawing a pink sewing machine surrounded by the words, "Strong Women Workers, but Only 6 Cents an Hour".

Each group takes their artifacts and attaches them to twine to form a clothesline. Each tells a story, each answers students' questions. Together, we string these clotheslines out around the classroom, creating a complicated network of paths, which forces us to interact with the artwork and writing. It reminds us of the photos of the clotheslines of the neighborhoods of major American cities—those that housed the garment sector nearly a century ago. And they are also reminiscent of the nests of wires that are haphazardly bursting from houses, high rises and telephone poles in places like Vietnam today. All are transmitting the stories of the workers, the people whose lives are too often hidden and obscured by the system of globalization that invites us to be unquestioning consumers.

Examining student-made artifacts.

With recent turmoil in worldwide markets, the fabric of a frayed system has begun to unravel, heightening the salience of studying and discussing the hidden costs of our consumption. Students in the United States and abroad are increasingly concerned about the human, environmental and economic impact of our choices.

Workers' lives are on the line—and when we make this visible, even at a small scale, we start to see the ties that bind us all together. It is these ties that remind us of the legacy of brave everyday people who have worked together to bring about a better world—and how we too can be proud contributors to this perennial endeavor.

Examining the clothesline.

The Role of Routines and the Concept of Emergence as a Method of Teaching with the Iron Rule

The rhythm starts with relationships of reciprocity: we listen, we respond and we synthesize. When we act in this manner, we model a dialogic style of learning that can drive inquiry, develop communication and bring a living element to classroom learning.

In the prior section of this chapter, I have given examples of units that use the AEIOU framework as means of following the "Iron Rule: don't do for others what they can do for themselves". These units addressed issues that started with noticing common things in our lives that are agitational: overflowing plastic bags in our cupboards and itchy tags on our shirts. The commonness of these issues lent them to explore both the immediate impact of the issue on our personal lives as well as broader applications of the issue in the community and world. The format of the units and teaching strategies deployed was also fairly common, which I hope provided those looking to take a small step toward teaching like an organizer ideas and encouragement. In the next section of this chapter, I would like to turn now to more open-ended methods of teaching and learning.

Open-end inquiry lends itself well to teaching like an organizer. Part of this is due to the fact that organizers operate with the understanding that they must use what they have. This can mean starting from scratch as an organizer. The organizer is reliant on tools like the one-on-one meeting, list making and issue tracking, public narrative and mountain modeling when starting from scratch. These tools, as I have tried to demonstrate, have relevance in the school setting as well.

Routine can further support the teacher-as-organizer. The teacher can create safety through fostering a sense of predictability by creating core activities that classes can revisit time and again. The class may be working on open-ended issues or in a setting, such as the outdoors, which has less physical constraints than the desk and chair brick and mortar classroom. In these cases, routine can increase the students' ability to know what's coming next and to know that there is an anchor activity that they will be returning to—a safe harbor, if you will.

Emergence

"You will be receiving clues about our first unit", I tell the class, "and it's your mission to figure out what the unit will be". First, I show them a video of a gray field bordered by leafless trees.

Slowly, a sound is building in the background. A dark cloud appears to descend over the field, shifting, forming one shape, maybe an oval and reforming into something else. It's a group of Starlings, but I don't say anything.

When the video ends and the Starlings have once again left the sky above the field, I ask "What do you think that was?" There are many ideas: bats, birds, shapeshifters….

"All good guesses, but you'll need more clues to find out about our first unit", I insist.

I pass out small slips of paper with stories that are 2–5 sentences in length. These are excerpts from adrianne marie brown's *Emergent Strategies* (2017). I ask the students to read the slips and create mini-posters related to their reading. The mini-posters should include a drawing that represents the story, a key-word or phrase from the story and a focus color.

Included in the collection are stories of: waves breaking on the shore with each wave being unique, a dandelion that was thought to be a weed, but was truly resilient and prolific in spreading its seeds, a group of birds that knew when it was time to migrate without being told, a stand of old oak trees that weathered a hurricane because their roots were intertwined and caterpillars that don't know that they will one day transform into beautiful butterflies, but it is their destiny.

It's the start of the year, so as I walk around the room and check-in with groups, I am looking at how the groups of students are talking with one another, working together or not. I am curious to see who wants to draw, who will read and who can bring their peers into the mix. Asking questions about each team's choices and stories, we are building our classroom.

While I still have the old-fashioned desks in my room that are attached to chairs, the desks are clustered in groups. Students stand up and I ask them to leave their mini-posters at their table group. Traveling together, they will rotate around the room visiting one another's posters, trying to gather more clues about the unit, searching for trends and commonalities.

These stories and this kind of work nudge us in the direction of collaboration, while providing nature-based allegories for our learning. We are the caterpillars, we are the dandelions, the waves, the Starlings and the oak trees. We are individuals and a community. We have to figure out how to trust ourselves and one another. And in doing so, we are moving toward being able to do for ourselves things that we couldn't do before.

This is a dynamic of being and becoming.

As a teacher, I experience my own discomfort with this dynamic daily. And this is the value of this small lesson and activity, we create visual anchors that remind us that we are not alone. In fact, what we are feeling is both natural and part of nature. Reminding ourselves of this, of the fact that we should trust our own nature and instincts when it comes to helping students develop greater self-direction, can help ease the anxiety that we may also be carrying from attempting to gently nudge our classrooms and schools toward a more humane style of education.

Setting the Table for Students to Lead

The only way that we can bridge the gap between the world as it is and the world as it should be is through finding more leaders. The leaders, I believe, are already here, they are our students. Yet, as leaders who are in the early learning stage of their development, our students are still discovering how to trust their senses. With this in mind, we can adopt the view of our classroom as a place where we can experience a kind of leadership development that starts with what is important to us. Having a place that invites us to identify and determine what is important, rather than being told what is important, is affirming. It is affirming of our past experiences and our ongoing development. It gives us the room to change our mind about issues and to gain new insights by being in conversation with one another. The Town Hall Meeting, which will be described next, is an example of a structure that we can use to support the important work of developing student judgment when it comes to assessing issues.

Town Hall Meetings

Each spring in New England, school gyms and cafeterias are turned into spaces for Town Hall meetings. These are meetings where citizens of the town weigh in on proposed budgets for the coming year and particular warrant articles, such as allocating money toward buying a new tanker truck for the Fire Department. Local officials and volunteers who serve on elected boards respond to questions about the proposals and the entire body of assembled citizens makes decisions for the community using a deliberative process.

In class, the deliberative Town Hall process can help students to learn to make decisions together. Setting up this style of meeting in class requires that you have as many desks or chairs as there are students. Create a semicircle of five desks and then make a line of 4–5 desks behind each of the desks in the semicircle. An aerial view of this desk configuration would look like a rising sun, with rays stretching out or half a bike wheel with spokes radiating out of the center. In setting up this configuration, make sure there is space to travel up and down each row.

Tell students that only the people in the front seat can speak. If you want to speak, tap the person sitting in the front seat on the shoulder and switch seats with them. The goal is to respond to one another, to listen to each other's questions and to reach a decision together through deliberation. Everyone is invited to come forward to speak during the conversation, and everyone is asked to keep track of the conversation through writing down notes on the discussion.

Coaching Tips for Town Hall Participation

When I coach students on participating in a Town Hall deliberation, I ask them if it's okay if the group starts with a shorter deliberation. I let them know that my goal is for the students to discuss with one another for the entirety of our established time goal. There are times when there might be awkward silence—and that's fine—it gives your peers time to think and process what they've heard, I assure them.

We might set a goal of being in deliberation for 5–7 minutes the first time. After the five minutes is up, I'll ask if everyone who wanted to speak was able to speak. I'll also ask what the group noticed about the conversation.

The most common trend that I've noticed is that students mostly state their own opinions and do not respond to or solicit the opinions of others initially. There are sometimes a few students who take up a lot of the airtime and other times when the group has students who are more reserved. This leads us to think about how we can involve more people in our deliberation and how we can ask one another questions to better explore ideas, rather than just stating what we may think. I will also suggest that students try to invite as many different people and views into the conversation as possible—that there is strength in diversity of opinion and viewpoints. In this regard, we define "winning" as involving everyone and trying our best to move away from simply stating what we believe or allowing viewpoints to go unexplored.

Next, I will keep trying to increase the amount of time we spend in the Town Hall. This can be done slowly over time—there is no rush. The next conversation move that I ask students to think about is how to "pivot" from one idea to another. Some students like to jump from one idea to the next and like the sense of control that comes with a pivot. When this happens, we can initially take a "time out" and ask how it feels to jump from one idea to another so quickly. Oftentimes, I hear students say that they feel frustrated because they didn't have enough time to think or respond— and that they were about to add something to the first idea before the discussion moved on.

Then comes the hard part, the class has to learn to "feel the discussion". Once the class has experienced the rushed pivot that feels like jumping from one idea to the next without continuity or conclusion, they are then challenged to find the right tempo for discussion—one that will allow for natural pauses for peers to think, collect their ideas and respond. Usually, having a particularly salient topic can help with this because students will want to stick to one idea for a longer period of time. I also suggest to students that when they are in the inner circle they can ask one another if anyone else has something to add to the current topic before we pivot to the next. This can result in a few people from the back of the line making their way up to the inner circle to get their comments and questions in before the conversation moves on.

The Town Hall Agenda

Throughout the week (or over the course of a couple of weeks) track issues that are agitating students to create an agenda for the Town Hall meeting. Your observations and notes from the week can be the basis of "hot topics" to discuss. There may be a few ongoing categories that these hot topics could be sorted into. It can also be helpful to have one-on-one conversations with students over the course of the week and ask them about the issues that they are having in class or in life. Assess your own comfort level on some of the topics and judge whether the classroom community is at a place where they can respectfully and thoughtfully take on certain topics.

Starting with easier topics can be a good way to build up the "civic muscle" or listening and responding to one another with care. Setting the agenda intentionally after speaking with students and soliciting their ideas gives everyone a sense of ownership and feeling heard. It can also allow you to redirect students if they need to talk with an adult (like you or a guidance counselor) about an issue. In this way, there is great power in the agenda to sift through issues, match students with resources, create a routine and form a workable progression for stretching our democratic skill of deliberation.

Deliberation is the practice of collectively solving issues. It is different from debate, in that it is not inherently adversarial. I group deliberation and debate under the larger umbrella of dialogue. Dialogue is simply a discussion between two or more people. Models of dialogue (including the one-on-one) have been sprinkled throughout this book. Dialogue and deliberation are mutually reinforcing practices. Groups that are committed to practicing dialogue and deliberation build trust in one another that allows for them to each work toward addressing tricky problems together. When we consider how each of these forms of communication can shape the classroom learning experience, we can make informed decisions about the next best move to building the "civic muscle" needed to make the easy and heavy lifts required in a democratic classroom and community. Scouting out the issues and potential categories for deliberation for our weekly agenda is how we can start to show that the democratic process can help us in solving problems together.

When "scouting" issues, having one-on-one conversations or soliciting topics for deliberation through other means (such as a letter drop-box or survey) it's important to be real about topic selection. Have the conversation up front about how topics will be selected and that not all topics may make their way into the Town Hall at first (and it's possible that some may never make their way into the forum). Reassure students that their contributions and suggestions are still important, even if a topic doesn't make its way into the forum. Reminding students of this periodically and also monitoring to make sure everyone feels like their voice is being heard are important to relationship building and also to overall classroom community cohesion.

Agenda Topics and Categories

The deliberative Town Hall meeting can address relevant seasonal issues. Students can help one another with problems on how to transition to a new school, an issue that comes up at the start and end of the year. Other students may have seasonal concerns like: the highs and lows of trying out for sports teams and plays, older siblings leaving for college or work and how to process school stress. Some students have spoken with parents, friends and family members about these issues already and they can draw on these conversations to provide advice and insight to their peers. Creating the kind of space where students can educate one another is a way of inviting those closest to the issue to have a voice in solving the issue. While some issues may seem too small—there can be big lessons learned in the small issues and a great chance to build confidence in deliberation.

Interpersonal issues can be one of the most relevant topics for classroom Town Hall discussions. There can be overlap between interpersonal issues and previously mentioned seasonal topics. In my view, the seasonal lens gives you a little more of a timeline and foresight into interpersonal issues that may "pop up". Classes that have more group work and more collaboration can see higher incidents of interpersonal conflict. We can use this as an opportunity to extend the curriculum and help students to learn deliberative skills that transfer to most learning and working settings.

Initiating a deliberation about an interpersonal issue should start with reminding students about your baseline rules and your purpose for deliberating. We are discussing this issue as an exercise in thinking through solutions that could work—not just for the members of our community who are experiencing this issue now, but also for anyone who might experience a similar issue in the future. This means that we have a responsibility to ourselves and our neighbors to bring our best ideas and questions to the circle. Then, we can set an agreed upon time and introduce the dilemma. You may want to distribute the agenda with the dilemma on it or post each individual dilemma/issue on the whiteboard or wall using a projector. It's helpful to have the visual reminder present for students to refer back to.

Starting the deliberation with a recurring question can ease students into the discussion with familiarity. It can also help students with introverted tendencies feel prepared entering into the discussion early on. One recurring issue is being listened to. I might say, "I am curious to know if everyone felt listened to this week in class. What worked?" Starting with what worked gives us a positive framing and invites students to share "wins".

After giving time for folks to respond, I'll introduce the second question of the sequence: What was tricky? This question takes a lot of trust to talk about—if your group isn't there yet, that's okay. Having the other elements of this deliberation and practicing staying in the "deliberation zone" can help us to build toward talking about the tricky issues, which in the end will help improve our solutions through directly addressing concerns. Still, it's fine to proceed to part three of this question sequence if your gut is telling you that your class isn't ready for direct discussion of what's tricky.

The third question in the sequence is: How do we do better?" This question orients us toward solutions and improving our practice as individuals and as a class. Again, using this similar framing can help to build familiarity and allow students to anticipate the question sequence and what's coming. This, in turn, can help them to anticipate how they might contribute to the conversation. Whatever solutions the class generated from their first deliberation can then be sorted during the next deliberation into the categories of "what's working' or "what's tricky". Following this pattern can help us to already have ideas about what we are "scouting" for in time between Town Hall meetings. It gives the opportunity for students to name their own focus points and to work at improving in those areas. This is part of the practice of what Deborah Meier (1995) called, "Schooling for ruling". In other words, the school experiences that we need to fully participate in the democratic project of self-rule.

Content-Related Town Halls

Another ongoing category for Town Hall discussion can be content-related questions. Similar to the other issues-based topics for town halls, when generating ideas for a content-related Town Hall deliberation think about being solution oriented. This can follow the challenge, choice, outcome framework discussed previously. Generally, we want to explore: What is the problem that was/is being faced? What was the range of options for addressing the problem? What was/is the best option for a solution? The following are examples of possible content-related question sequences for deliberation:

Example question sequences for historical content

Challenge: Why did the colonies want to leave the British Empire?
Choice: What choices did the colonies have?
Outcome: Was the outcome worth the cost?

Example question sequence for geographic content

Challenge: Were there challenges or surprises that we ran into while mapping the wetlands this week?
Choice: What places could we have explored that went unexplored? Should we have avoided certain areas?
Outcome: How could we have approached the mapping in a different way that would have made better use of our time?

Example question sequence for science content

Challenge: How are our lakes being affected by invasive species?
Choice: What could be done to lessen the impact of invasives?
Outcome: Which solution would be most likely to be accepted by our community?

A layer to consider adding to the Town Hall when you are discussing content is viewpoint. This can look similar to the plastic presser discussed earlier in this chapter where you post the content-related problem, brainstorm who is/was affected by the issue and represent that viewpoint at the Town Hall. Of course, this requires consideration of the problem and viewpoints. One way to approach the issue of viewpoint representation is to ask students to be content experts from whatever particular field of study (history, science, seismology, journalism, etc.) and provide them with the stem: "I am a (historian) who is looking into the issue of _____ exploring the perspective of_____". Students can then gather evidence from credible sources that help to explore their chosen perspective. This approach can create a tone of "professional" inquiry for the meeting. It can also coincide with a discussion of how to represent and discuss varied viewpoints in relation to evidence. Concepts such as objectivity and subjectivity can also be valuable teaching lessons that come from exploring viewpoints through content.

Current events are another category of questions that can be used to relate content and deliberation. It's important to acknowledge that the news can too often make us feel debilitated—that the world is all doom and gloom. This is why many families have tried to shield their children from the news. There is also the ongoing polarization in the news-media ecosystem. These tangible factors increase the reticence of some who might otherwise engage with current events in the classroom. Yet, there is such relevance to the daily developments of our world, which means that we should at least wrestle with the methods that we could use to include current events in our classroom discussions.

For me, Town Hall deliberation is a productive avenue for the inclusion of current events in the curriculum because of the solution-oriented nature of deliberation. This can be especially true when using school and local news. There are issues being discussed locally like whether to hire more trash collectors, whether to add a sidewalk along a busy street, or if we should expand public pre-school. All of these topics ask us to define the challenge, explore the range of choices and try to come to a solution that the classroom community (and then the larger community) feels like benefits the most people. Engaging students in working to find common ground on these issues not only prepares them for future participation in local life, it allows them to enter today—talking with family members and neighbors about these issues. It's a foot onto the ladder of engagement for students and a step toward doing more for themselves and their community.

Our approach to gathering and sorting through stories can help to tailor topics to student interests. In weeks where you will discuss current events, it can be helpful to survey or ask students which events they are really interested in discussing. Depending on our class's age, we can provide student-friendly news sources and ask them to recommend articles that might interest the whole class. Alternatively, if students vote on or identify a current event topic we can locate a short article that the class can review together, which can help to ground the conversation. Discussing current events without a common article to base the discussion can be hazardous because there will be a lot of secondhand commentary. Reviewing one article together can give everyone a clear starting place for discussion. Reading an article out aloud with the class can pay off, even if it may take a little more time up front. Once students have heard your question sequences a few times, you can also invite them to contribute their own questions to help guide the deliberation.

Town Hall deliberations increase student agency in the classroom. We can help to build student familiarity with deliberation by practicing routines, such as structuring question sequences. When students see the predictability of deliberative discussion, they can prepare to participate in a way that meets their needs. The cooperative nature of deliberation reinforces the need to hear and value all viewpoints in the room. This can be encouraging for our students who may be reticent to participate in other forms of classroom discussion. Furthermore, the Town Hall deliberation asks students who are comfortable with participating to invite their peers into the conversation and to learn how to create their own community space that sustains dialogue. In this respect, the Town Hall deliberation offers differentiation that exemplified the meaning of the "iron rule" in the classroom. It takes time and practice to refine our deliberation skills, but this style of conversation is a cornerstone of a self-directed class, in that it democratizes the problem identification, solution creation process.

Conclusion

The Iron Rule of organizing can feel scary when we start to practice it in the classroom. Yet, the rule, which instructs us to "not do for others what they can do for themselves" fits well with our goal as teachers. We want students to learn independence and self-regulation. We want students to feel the self-confidence that comes from knowing that you can now do something that you could not do before. This means giving students the chance to try things out, to mess up, to reflect and to try again. Seeing this in practice, even in a small way, gives students and teachers the confidence that self-directed learning does not mean being abandoned on the mountainside all alone. In fact, it means that we will be finding ways to support student learning that help them keep climbing toward their "mountain top" goals.

Reaching our mountain top goals requires that we understand the terrain of our learning. There is going to be a steep part of our climb. This means being prepared and it means using pace. As teachers, we can feel the pace of learning and use our teacher tools to gear students up for the ascent. One of the tools that we have that can help us build the kind of momentum needed for both steep ascents and for bridging the challenging chasms of learning is the ladder of engagement. Planning out our use of activities to save energy, to maintain energy and to create bursts of engagement that move us toward new peaks of collective action and inquiry is essential.

Pairing the ladder of engagement with the mountain model allows us the flexibility to move toward a more self-directed style of teaching. We can use the model as a planning tool for ourselves, as a communication tool with students and even as a tool for students to take on planning some of their own learning. All of these options are also complimented when the mountain model is used for reflection. We can look back on the work and learning that we've done and think about the changes that we could make when we approach the next climb.

The AEIOU framework is another important tool to use as we plan our units. The framework helps us to think iteratively as teachers about how to respond to the needs of students without "doing the work for them". We are teaching as organizers when we anticipate the need to agitate, when we structure peer-to-peer educational dialogues, when we inspire students to keep going even as they know that tough parts are coming, when we facilitate students matching the jobs that need to be done with their interests and talents, and when we uplift student learning in ways that make them feel appreciated. Each element of the AEIOU framework can be modeled by teachers for students and can be transferred to students who are ready to lead on their own. The AEIOU framework can also be overlaid onto Town Hall deliberations. It's my hope that the deliberation conversation stems and question sequences show how we can model and transfer collaborative and solution-oriented discussion to students to increase their agency and democratic skills. All of this relates back to the important point that we, as teachers, have the power to read our classrooms, listen to our students and make the next best move in determining what works best for the path that we are on in creating a more self-directed and democratic classroom.

Works Cited

ABC News (Australia). (2021, February 23). Supermarket confronts customers about plastic waste. | ABC News. YouTube. https://www.youtube.com/watch?v=v7Jj3LcDWgA

Bradbury, A., Brenner, M., & Slaughter, J. (2016). *Secrets of a successful organizer*. Labor Notes Brown, Adrienne Maree. *Emergent Strategy*. AK Press.

Meier, D. (1995). *The power of their ideas: Lessons for America from a small school in Harlem*. Beacon Press.

Levey, S. (2015, September 1). *Health of seabirds threatened as 90 per cent swallow plastic | Imperial News | Imperial College London*. Imperial News. https://www.imperial.ac.uk/news/167386/health-seabirds-threatened-90-cent-swallow/

MASS MoCA. (2024, June 6). *The Plastic Bag Store*. YouTube. https://www.youtube.com/watch?v=Ool9Hcon0H0

NPR. "PEOPLE: Planet Money Makes a T-Shirt (Part III)." *YouTube*, 5 Dec. 2013, www.youtube.com/watch?v=-6T1MvHyUic

Paul, M., & Zunon, E. (2017). *One plastic bag: Isatou Ceesay and the recycling women of the Gambia*. Scholastic Inc.

Riis, J. A. (1890). Charles Scribner's Sons. *How the other half lives: Studies among the tenements of New York*. Charles Scribner's Son.

Rogers, C. R. (1969). *Freedom to learn*. Merrill.

Right Question Institute. (2018). *What is the QFT?* Right Question Institute. https://rightquestion.org/what-is-the-qft/

UNC-Chapel Hill. (2018, September 18). *The Plastic Bag Store*. YouTube. https://www.youtube.com/watch?v=hemPPkjH62g

Wiggins, G., & McTighe, J. (2005). *Understanding by design* (2nd ed.). Association for Supervision and Curriculum Development.

5
Make Connections Locally

Deep Organizing: Roots and Rocks

Deep organizing asks us to come into sustained relationships over time in one place—to sink down into the culture of one place. As a teen, my dad had me take a post hole digger to sink posts down into the ground. We would mix a bag of quick-crete with water and pour the mixture down into the hole surrounding the base of the post. It would take a few hours for the quick-crete to dry and for the post to set, but sure enough it held steady.

When you dig down in New England soil, you're likely to find two things: rocks and roots. I think digging down into rooty rocky soil applies well to deep organizing too. Spend long enough in a place and you'll discover your roots and those of the people around you too. You'll also find yourself wedged between some tough rocks, the issues that make life a little difficult and that you might not have a shared vision for approaching with your neighbors. You can use those rocks when you're digging post holes, they can help close the gap between the post and hole, giving a bit more structure to your work. And I think that's the case for deep organizing as well, it works to have issues that can't just be swept away. When we're done digging those hard issues can help shore things up—helping us to leave things better than we found it. It's the rocky parts that help build something that will last. They create a little structure and tension for building community.

Teaching like an organizer, we come to know our students, their roots and the issues that are meaningful to their lives. Their roots extend into the communities surrounding our schools. We develop our judgment for using issues in our teaching over time. Time teaches us ways to scaffold our projects using both the roots (relationships) and the rocks (issues). We test our effectiveness when we dig down into our communities and gain firsthand experience. Committing to this adventure, to exploring the common things that are unknown, is the path toward teaching like an organizer.

"Deep organizing" has become a common phrase in the organizing world. The idea is that we're not developing relationships for transactional purposes. While there is a range of depths in terms of the relationships that we have in our lives, we are building relationships to have stronger schools where every student feels known, neighborhoods where we watch out for one another and communities where we all strive to help one another to grow the common good.

The idea of this kind of long-term relationship building was something that just happened naturally when I was growing up in a small town in New England. It was common for multiple generations of neighbors to live and work together—grandparents had served on school boards or planning boards together. An uncle had worked at the quarry where granite for a school house foundation was hauled. Communal activity and relationships were a fact of life because each person depended on the other to make it through the winter, all while also maintaining a fierce streak of independence and pride.

Thinking back, my small town New England upbringing was very common, especially from the point of view of an organizer. If someone had parachuted in from a different state or different region and told us what needed to be fixed about our sleepy little town and how to do the fixing, the person wouldn't have been given the time of day.

"Now, why is that?" we might ask. Maybe the person had fresh eyes, a new perspective and valid points that could have helped everyone in the community have a better life. That could be true. At the same, it says something about the local community if they have been living all their lives with a problem and have been unable to recognize the problem or unable to solve it. The problem-solving newcomer can be perceived taking away agency from the long-time locals and disrespecting their experiences, priorities and choices. By placing a "program" ahead of the people, the newcomer is advancing a paternalistic theory of change, which places the locals in the position of receivers of services—rather than independent neighbors capable of solving their own problems together.

> "If you have come here to help me you are wasting your time, but if you have come because your liberation is bound up with mine, then let us work together".
> —Lila Watson, artist and activist

When we teach like an organizer, we recognize that working with young people can place us in the position of being the problem-solving newcomer. Some classes might want us to fill that role. The key is for us to be connected with our class through one-on-one conversations to be able to determine the best path forward in our development as a classroom community.

As teachers, we can identify problems for students. This is a common approach that can be very effective. We can provide a range of solutions to the problems that we identify. And we can coach students to determine which solutions might make the most sense, asking them to support their reasoning. All these teaching moves are practical methods. And our challenge is to reflect as teacher organizers and to see if we can move closer toward an ideal where students can take even more of an active role in learning together in creating a better world, honoring their independence and also the power of their relationships.

Two Levels of Organizing: The Inside and Outside Game

The school year provides guideposts for relationship development. It is typical for our classroom communities to span just one academic year or possibly two, if we loop with students.

We might call our anticipated time together our "timelines of togetherness". One or two years is a short amount of time in the span of a career or in the span of our time living in a community. This presents a challenge for the teacher-as-organizer, concurrent levels of organizing: the "inside game" and the "outside game".

The "inside game" is the organizing within our own classrooms with our students. The time frame is determined by the school year and the seasons define our interaction with place, especially in climates where there are distinct seasons. Much of this book has been about the "inside game" of teaching as an organizer, so I will now turn to the "outside game".

The "outside game" of teaching as an organizer is more expansive, both in its timeline and in the people it seeks to involve. The "outside game" has a timeline that spans the duration of our teaching careers. The reason for this long view is that every relationship that you create with members of the community at large is a potential resource for your class or a gateway to other resources. Each person is connected to other people and each person is connected to the place they live in. This means almost unlimited chances to connect, reconnect and come into a deeper relationship with the broader community that surrounds our school.

The contrast between the timelines for the "inside game" and "outside game" of teaching like an organizer has potential for conflict. As teachers, we want to bring learning to life with the most relevant, interesting and dynamic connections to the community. The vision of seamless connection between classroom and broader community meets the reality of availability, funding for transportation or supplies and hurdles presented by various forms of paperwork. These constraints are real and can have the effect of giving us a diminished sense of agency on the short-term horizon. That's where having the long-term viewpoint of linking the "inside" and "outside" game can help strengthen our resolve. While the short-term view can motivate us to action, the long-term view can give us the patience we need not only to create connections, but also to forge partnerships.

Stepping toward the Unknown: Interviews and Building Out the Circle of Community

Once students have experienced exploring the local area—it may be time to expand our vision of community. One of the best places to start locally is to use interviews. Interviewing the custodian, groundskeeper or food service worker at your school can provide students with a chance to find out more about the inner workings of the school. Students want to know things like: Where does the trash go? How much trash do we have each day? How long does it take to sweep all the floors? How long have you been working here? Do you listen to music when you work? What is in the custodian's closet and how big is the school freezer? All of these questions bring us closer to knowing how a school keeps going. These kinds of questions and interviews let students and staff get to know one another better. They can also be a journey within the school building for students—a journey into the world of the unknown aspects of school life—an extension of the lived experiences of the learners.

Photo of student interviewing a staff member.

To build out interview experiences start with the extended staff who keep schools running, then consider surveying parents and creating a list of parent's interests and expertise (as mentioned in Chapter 1). This would then allow you or students to reach out to parents for interviews or for help to make community connections as the year progresses.

You never know who will have a connection to class. One year, a parent spoke to our class about her time working for the Red Cross in Tajikistan where she helped to distribute over a million meals. In our interconnected world, there are so many stories that connect us to both places and people far away and down the street. Interviews can help us make these connections.

Photo of a mother presenting to class.

Engaging staff members and parents in the inquiry projects of your class builds a greater understanding among students and adults about what the classroom is all about. In the process, it reduces the divide between adults and children. It reminds students that we all have something to teach and something to learn.

What Is a Community Partner?

Surfacing possible community partners takes time, patience and forethought. Consider what you'll be teaching and how an expert from the community could enhance the learning. Also, think about what folks in your school building have done in the past. Chances are high that someone has connections that you can use or build off of. There is no need to start from scratch. To help us think about community partnerships, it's important to note that not all partnerships are the same—and that's okay. We have different classroom needs, different curricular requirements and there are many other pressures that shape what we can do with partners. To help us think about the kinds of partnerships and choices we may make in developing or pursuing those partnerships, it can be helpful to sort partnerships into categories. The three identifiable partnerships categories are: the guest, the field observation and the reciprocal relationship.

The guest partner is a great entry point for creating bonds with the community. The guest can share their knowledge with students or demonstrate skills that are relevant to a study. This could be via a digital interface, like Zoom. It could also involve the person physically sharing space in the classroom with the students. Inviting guests to perform music or art can enhance student cultural appreciation. Guests are generally a more convenient option for the teacher and students, in that the guest is appearing at the school, and for the most part, appears within the school day. The guest speaker or guest exhibitor is a great way to start to foster community connection.

Past Examples of Guest Partners

- School custodians
- School administrators
- School Food Service Worker
- School Paraprofessionals
- Town Clerk
- Lowe's Manager
- Red Cross Foreign Aid Worker
- Former Police Commissioner
- Catholic Charities Attorney
- Immigration Rights Advocate
- Photographer
- Local farmer
- Grandfather and historian of the Holocaust
- Former President of regional NAACP
- Local Firefighter
- Local Police
- Local actress
- Grandmother and conservationist
- Regional Conservation Association
- Local Church Affiliates
- High school students
- A mom who raised chickens

The field observation requires students and teachers to move outside their school building to visit sites that are related to their study. Visiting sites where adults practice solving community issues provides students with a window into the relevance of their school inquiries. This can help students to think more deeply about the subject of their inquiries.

As teachers, we can further increase the salience of learning in partnership with community members when students can have a firsthand experience with a partner in the community. From the teacher's perspective, there is more planning involved in coordinating a field observation with a partner: arranging transportation, planning the experience with the partner, collecting money and documenting permission forms. Using field observations to get students out into the community to experience firsthand what it's like to see experts work on issues is a fantastic step to creating deeper community partnerships.

Reciprocal partnerships are mutually beneficial. They are partnerships where students can contribute meaningfully to the work of the partners and where partners can contribute to student learning. These partnerships can take many different forms. There are reciprocal partnerships that are oriented toward service learning, that are oriented toward student mentorship and that are oriented toward public engagement. These elements of reciprocal learning can be fluid and one experience can blend multiple elements together. Describing reciprocal partnerships and adding to our awareness of the range of possible opportunities can help to define our own purpose for pursuing particular partnerships. Knowledge of the different reciprocal partnerships can also help us to weave different elements into the student experience.

Service can be a meaningful element of partnerships. Service places students in the role of aiding the mission of community partners. This is an especially powerful experience when students learning about an issue can be connected to serving in their own community. Connecting service to learning in the curriculum differentiates it from service as volunteerism. Service learning can include direct or indirect service with the community partner. Direct service includes working with a partner's client(s) or working alongside a partner's staff on tangible actions. Indirect service involves students participating in tasks that support the broad mission of the partner, for example providing research support, data collection or analysis in collaboration with the partner.

Reciprocal or Site Visit?

The following are past projects. Are they site visits or examples of reciprocal partnerships?

- Traveling to a citizenship naturalization ceremony
- Distributing *Street Sheet* to the public, a newspaper about homelessness written by folks experiencing homelessness
- Stocking shelves at the community pantry
- Cleaning headstone in a cemetery
- Picking up trash on the highway
- Visiting a public health clinic to speak with providers
- Conducting a voter registration drive
- Visiting an immigrant aid non-profit organization to learn about access to housing and legal assistance for those new to the country
- Running a bingo game at an assisted living center for the elderly and listening to the resident stories
- Weeding a community garden and learn about pollinators
- Going to the library, getting a tour and signing all the students up for library cards

Gears to Gardens Mural and bench in the Pilsen neighborhood of Chicago, site of our service in 2019.

Mentorship can be an important part of a community partnership. Community partnerships connect students to people who are working on all kinds of important work in the community. We are building a community network for students when we introduce new people and organizations through learning in partnership. The result can be students spending more time working with the partner in the short term, for example, volunteering afterschool at the library or animal shelter. Partnerships also build familiarity for students that can lead them to return to work with partner organizations in the future. These benefits are in addition to the immediate benefits of partners mentoring students and modeling their approach and craft during curricular projects.

Community partnerships present an avenue for public engagement. Traveling to a site to work with staff and clients of community partners places students in conversation with the public. These meetings can be mutually beneficial—students hear what it's like to be an adult involved with a public issue and the adults hear the perspective of young people on issues that are relevant to their lives and work. This intergenerational dialogue is part of the reweaving of the civic fabric of our communities.

Reciprocal partnerships that are sustained over time are more likely to address the needs of both partners. Both partners become more familiar with the needs of one another, more familiar with the issues present and more familiar with supporting one another. Many issues require sustained work over time to resolve. Long-term partnerships can translate into systematic approaches to working together to address an issue. Alternatively, there can be a cycle of churn and turnover that takes time away from the community partner and time away from the teacher. Nurturing partnerships to make sure that both parties are getting what they need requires revisiting our purpose for working together. That purpose may shift over time or our needs may change. In either case, we can check-in and make sure that we continue to be on the same page when it comes to working together.

Your Credential and Introductory Outreach

Getting started with forming a community partnership of any kind starts with what you and your students hope to accomplish. From there, you can list out the different connections that you already have in the community that could be potential partnerships. Ask your coworkers and existing local connections to help you to identify other people in the community who you might want to reach out to about a partnership project.

Our job title of "teacher" is a critical credential. Whether walking up to a store front to talk with a local business owner, writing an email or making a call, our title as "teacher" will unlock doors. Folks generally want to help schools out and when they have the chance to share their knowledge, skill or general experience—they jump at the chance. Starting your outreach by clearly identifying yourself as a teacher will help you build connections.

It's also important to explain why you feel like any person would be a good fit as a partner. Tell your potential partner the gist of the project and what you hope they can contribute. Sometimes, folks have experience speaking with students or have children themselves, and other times they have limited experience with young people. In either case, it can be reassuring when we offer to help and provide guidance on sharing with your grade level. While they are the experts on their issues and topics—we are the experts on our students. Finally, provide the times and dates for scheduling. Reaching out in advance of a unit will give you a better chance to schedule a time and date for collaborating with a partner.

Example Introductory Email

Mrs. Singer,

My name is Jacob Goodwin and I'm a sixth grade teacher at the Cooperative Middle School in Exeter. Our class will be studying globalization this year. We would love for you to visit our school and share your knowledge of the history of the mills in our community. If you are open to coming in and presenting, I am happy to help "workshop" your presentation, if that would be helpful. You would be speaking to groups of 20-ish students throughout the day. I am currently looking at dates in the last week of March. We truly appreciate your consideration and I think the students will learn a great deal from your experience.

Thank you,
Jacob
Cell: (- - -) - - - - - - - -
Email address:

Where Can We Look for Community Partners?

List building is a key part of organizing. Lists are where we can keep names and contact information for community partners. It's also where we can keep information on potential leads, notes on past experiences and questions for future work. As I've mentioned previously, list building can start with the families who are connected to the students in our classrooms. Keeping a list of your own allows you to refer back to contacts years later. Rather than depending on the record keeping of others, you are in control of your own data. But where can you look for community partners beyond parents and families?

Public service providers can be a great source of community partnerships. This includes: libraries, police, fire, EMT (emergency medical technician), clinics, various departments and outreach programs of public universities, museums, public works, town or municipal administrative offices, various local boards (select boards, planning boards, zoning boards, etc.), household waste and recycling centers, political offices (especially ones that offer constituent services) and local non-profits and associations. All of these sources of potential partners have contact information that is easily obtained through a quick search of the web.

Local fairs, celebration and civic gatherings can also be good places to surface community partners. In New Hampshire, many of the larger events of this kind are in the summer and fall. This is mostly a function of our climate. Knowing the cycle of the celebrations and events in your area can help you plan for attending and collecting information that you can bring back to your class. Use the one-on-one conversation technique to get a sense of different vendors' interests in working with schools and helping connect young people to their line of work.

Not everyone is interested—read the situation, value your time and the time of potential partners. Asking the worker of a fried dough stand for anything other than an order of fried dough when it's peak business hours will likely result in a hard "no".

Find the "yes" at the event, get their contact information, add the contact info to your list of potential partners and follow up with them in a timely manner. This can mean sending a short email saying, "nice to meet you". Even if you don't immediately plan an engagement with the contact, your outreach shows that you are a person who is thoughtful and interested in making connections.

Keeping up to date on event offerings at local libraries, universities and associations can help produce leads as well. These types of civic institutions host guest speakers of their own—both people who live in the community and experts who may be traveling in from elsewhere. Attending events, asking questions and going up and introducing yourself after to the speakers can help you further build out your resource network. With digital conference calls like Zoom today, there is always a chance that an expert who lives further away may still be open to "calling" into class for a project. Personally, I find the conversations more fruitful and the relationship potential much greater when folks can visit the classroom in person and when they live in the area. That said, there is value in adding new perspectives to the mix, especially when it helps us understand where we live better.

Keep in mind your curriculum and how it flows throughout the year. Prioritizing partnerships that link to upcoming projects can help you to move ahead on partnerships rather than simply stockpiling contact info. Acting on one contact, starting to develop the relationship and enhancing student learning is better than having a hundred business cards sitting in your desk drawer. This is the key to organizing: acting.

If after contacting any of these organizations and people, it seems that they might not be the right fit for what you're trying to do, you can always ask them to refer you to someone else. Oftentimes, it's the referral that ends up being the person or group that works out. Don't give up. Work your leads, document your progress, including when you have dead ends. You never know, a "no" today can turn into a future "yes".

Coding your list of community contacts can help you keep track of how partnerships are developing. Using a simple color-coding system can be an easy way to track whether partnerships are on pause (red), moving slowly toward being integrated into the curriculum (yellow) or are currently integrated (green). Color-coding gives you a quick way to sort through contacts and gives you an idea of where the partnerships are heading and what kinds of action might help you move the partnership in the right direction. It can also be helpful to use a tab on the bottom of Excel or Google Sheets to create separate contact lists for different issues. Writing down the times when you communicate with community partners on the list keeps you thinking about your patterns of communication and if you need to follow up with a partner.

Examples of Community Partnerships in Practice

Having discussed methods for scouting and tracking partnerships, as well as different models for community partnerships, now let's turn toward examples of what community partnerships look like in practice. In this section, I will be highlighting different classrooms and grades that each have practiced different types of community partnerships. Here, I've aimed to include partnerships that are rooted in the immediate human, natural and built world. While your context may differ, there are likely elements of each example that you can try out and then refine. These teachers have put in the work to create guest partnerships that invite community members into their schools, site-based partnerships for observational visits and reciprocal partnerships that support both student learning and the work of the partner. The range of partnerships demonstrates the adaptability of the practice of place-based learning. Rooted in our local areas, it can bring communities together to share in the work of improving the community.

Guest Partner Example

In my first year of teaching, one of the topics in the thick curriculum binder that I had been given was the Dust Bowl. Unsure of how to make the topic of top soil erosion interesting for students, I decided to follow my gut and started with the food that we eat. The school where I worked at the time was small and served grade K through eight in a rural setting. The physical building included a portable classroom in the front parking lot, a newer middle school annex with a gym and the older elementary wing, which had a small library at one end the main entrance and a cafeteria at the other end. It was in the cafeteria where I started to scout out the inquiry project.

I noticed that many students who received the school lunch threw away the fruits that accompanied their meals in the large trash bins lined with thick black bags scattered throughout the room. I noticed Pizza was the most popular meal. And I noticed that the food service team was not under the restrictions of my previous school, which had gone "pork free" to accommodate students' religious practices.

Armed with the monthly menu and my observations, I read the menu to my classes of seventh graders. "What's the best day to get school lunch?" I asked, confirming the high interest in Pizza. "What's the day you most fear?" I followed up, with a twinkle in my eye. The class erupted—and my young-teacher-self was taken aback by the volcanic responses that included "overcooked green beans". "Hmmm..." I mused aloud, "Would it surprise you to know that there was a time in America when all sorts of crops were wiped out and when kids like you had nearly no choices for lunch at all?"

I could read the skepticism on their faces. They largely thought I was trying to guilt them into eating the overcooked green beans. I was not.

"It was called the Dust Bowl," I concluded, "and before we learn about it, I want to think about food here–at our school. How do we improve on the overcooked green beans?" Relieved to not be guilt-tripped into eating more soggy veggies and not to be at the receiving end of a long lecture on the Dust Bowl, the class was full of suggestions for improving the lunch experience at school.

While I didn't know it at the time, I had wandered into issue organizing. The students had many ideas on what contributed to the overall lunch quality, in fact they had a much larger view than I had considered in my observations. Students thought of sourcing food, its preparation, its cost, the way these factors made the cafeteria staff who prepared it feel and what happened to the food when it went uneaten. All of these issues became topics for student research.

They wanted to know about composting, about growing food in gardens and local farms. We traveled back to the cafeteria to get a closer look at patterns related to our food. The lunches were somewhat staggered in the day, which allowed different classes to monitor what was being thrown away—a data point of interest to students in multiple groups.

Next, students identified the cook and manager of the cafeteria, a veteran who ran a tight ship, as a person to interview. Generously, she agreed to talk with students after the morning breakfast was served one day. I didn't want her to feel like we were disrespecting her work, she was trying to feed a few hundred kids on a shoestring budget. She was very matter of fact about what went into planning and ordering the food. "The federal government had a large role in the cafeteria's offerings", she said (something that I made a mental note of for later comparisons with the Dust Bowl).

Students took notes and tried to pull together the data that they gathered from the cafeteria along with survey data and researched facts from our use of the school's mobile computer lab. They formatted their work in the form of a proposal: a general research question, a hypothesis, a summary of the problem, a description of the data they gathered, their analysis of costs and benefits and a conclusion.

Talking with my colleague, the reading teacher, about the topic, she suggested that I try to connect with a local farmer. She had a friend who could help. After a few emails and a brief chat on the phone, the farmer came in before school to talk about his role as a guest—and how we might work together. He was enthusiastic about the student's interest in sustainability and local agriculture, a passion of his own. I could relate, my parents had farmed in Northern New Hampshire for a period in the 1960s and 1970s, with my mom returning to farming later with her second husband. We shared a common bond in this way. Still, the farmer was a practical man, the land in our Granite State has a way of making practical men out those who try to eke out an existence from its rocky soil.

He wanted to know if students' interest was real or if it was "just another school project". I, a "green" teacher, lacking the seasoning that hard times in a profession impart at that point in my career, misunderstood his question, taking it to be condemnation of my earnest attempt to create a relevant experience with the students. Unsure of how to answer, and not wanting to appear ungrateful for his time, or even worse have him walk out before class started, I didn't object to the project being "just another school project". Instead, I listened and then we went over the agenda for his participation in class. Students started arriving and it was time to start the school day.

The day went off without a hitch. I had cut out questions that students had prepared the days before for the farmer and for one another based on their research. I grouped desks together and placed 2–3 paper question strips at each desk group. Each group of students would pick up the questions, ask a question and discuss what they thought. In this way, everyone had a chance to talk about their work with students from other groups. After seven minutes, students would stand up and move to another table group that had a different set of questions. The farmer sat at one of the desk groups throughout the period and responded to the students' questions. The set up for this "conversation cafe" was the farmer's idea—and he ended it with a general question and answer session for the last 15 minutes of class.

I thanked the farmer after the last class of the day. He headed back to the farm. I rearranged the desk, thinking about the project. The students had enjoyed sharing their questions and ideas with the farmer and hearing what he had to say about the range of topics, including the prospects of a school compost pile. Beneath the relief of making it through my first day with a guest in class, I felt a gnawing feeling. I couldn't help but wonder if I had done the right thing in not defending the project to the farmer. I wanted him to say that the project was real—but he had chickens to feed and chores to do. The practicalities of life for him meant constant motion, unrelenting responsiveness to the short growing season and the ever-present challenges posed by beetles, bugs and various rodents that threatened his crops.

The farmer was inescapably in the "world as it is". Yet, here he was, in a classroom of a new teacher, spending some of his valuable time having a one-on-one conversation with me and holding small group conversations with students. He listened carefully to our issues and challenged us to "make it real". He didn't insist that we open a greenhouse tomorrow and start growing all our own food, even some of our simple ideas were maybe too idealistic to him. He wanted us to join him in the "world as it is"—and in so doing be methodical about the seeds we planted, the ideas we tended and the tomorrow that we were growing toward. The farmer was organizing us. The farmer's lesson challenged me to teach like an organizer.

Inviting guests from the community into our classrooms and schools brings new ideas into the fold, both for students and teachers. As a new teacher, it sounds naive, but I had the belief that things would just work out. I hadn't experienced the harsh truth that experience teaches us: things often don't work out and that we should treasure those times when things do break in our favor. The very fact that the farmer was there, in my classroom, and not in the field, was a testament to his hope for our partnership. And he had to temper that hope by reminding me that our best laid plans can result in barren fields. What I had to learn for myself, which I couldn't articulate at the time, was that things also become real when we try, even if we come up short. That young people, teachers and students, need to see the messiness that comes with trying things out. In that messiness of trying, failing, adapting and trying again, we learn about the "realness" of the world, the "realness" of our projects and the "realness" of ourselves. That is something that we can never learn from canned curriculum or guests who stick to a script and who try to not offend the teacher.

We take a step into the unknown when we bring guests into our classrooms. It is that risk that sharpens our minds and brings us to focus on their words. The newness of the speaker, the difference between their daily experience and our own, engages the part of our mind that asks, "what could be?" It's not only a question about the future, but also a question that asks us to use our imagination. It's a generative question. Based on what this new person is sharing, we successively ask: What other ways of living exist in our community? How can their experience help me to make sense of my life? What does this new knowledge mean for what I'm currently doing? Each of these questions has immediate and deep relevance to the learner. Each of these questions is surfaced through "newness"—in experience and in personality. The teacher-as-organizer uses the newness of the guest to increase the salience of the topic at hand, inviting the learner to imagine and assess. This is the duality invited by guests.

There is also a simple lesson within the story of the farmer: setting clear expectations for guests can help everyone. There are many people in the community who are eager to engage young people. Expressing to those visitors not only the aspirations for student projects, but also as one sixth grader once told me, "Not all seeds make their way to the ground. Not all ideas bloom" (Goodwin, 2024). When community guests understand that student learning and student projects are susceptible to the natural forces that govern the growth of all things, there is a greater empathy for the student learning process. From this empathy flows the relationship that can truly nurture growth.

Preparing for Guests

Prior to the day of the speaking engagement, I'll let the speaker know the parking situation and how and where to check into the school. I also let them know that a delegation of students will wait for them at the main office and show them down to the classroom. These are all little logistical details that help create a welcoming experience for our guests.

Whenever a guest speaker visits, I ask the speaker to send us a short biography that we can use to introduce him/her. I'll split the biography into a few smaller sections—as short as one sentence. This gives several students a chance to introduce the speaker, standing in front of the class with the printed out biography. As much as possible, I try to be in the background and have the students lead the guest visits. Again, I let the speaker know this in advance.

Oftentimes, we print out a rough timeline for the visit and have a student facilitate the conversation with the speaker. For example, we might have: (1) Welcome and introduction, (2) speaker presentation and (3) student question and answer. During the student question and answer, the student facilitator will call on students to ask questions, listening to the question carefully to make sure that the guest speaks to the question. If the guest misses a part of the question, the facilitator can respectfully follow up. In preparing for speakers, I'll ask each student to prepare an index card that states something that they have recently been learning related to the guest's experience and a question.

One year, in our unit studying historical changemakers, a student asked the former President of the Seacoast NAACP (National Association for the Advancement of Colored People), Mr. Rogers Johnson, a question based on their research of the Tuskegee Airmen:

Index Card Question

Recently, I was learning about the obstacles overcome by the Tuskegee Airmen. The Airmen had to fight racism both at home and abroad.

Where do changemakers get their bravery?

Mr. Johnson took the students' question with great respect and care. He spoke about the historical importance of the Tuskegee Airmen in the context of the war and in the context of American history. He then encouraged the students to find the bravery that existed in each one of them and reminded them that bravery had to be grown over time—that it had to be practiced.

It's special when intergenerational dialogue takes root between guest partners and students. Mr. Johnson visited our school in back-to-back years, before his passing. Each time, students would go up to him at the end of our period together and want to tell him more or ask him a question. His generosity in sharing his experience was palpable. He spoke of being a young person, being a big baseball fan and moving from New York to New Hampshire and the difficulty of being "the new kid". His stories were relatable to the students and put them in conversation with a local changemaker.

Guest partners from the community help students to develop a more robust sense of place. Our ability to relate to place through the stories of those who have lived here before grants us access to lived knowledge gained through experience. It also gives us a path toward criticality. Civil rights activist and Harvard lecturer Marshall Ganz defines criticality as a "combination of a critical eye and a hopeful heart that brings change". Our direct contact with our neighbors and members of the local community is naturally fertile ground for many questions about place, about ourselves and about the relationship between the natural and human world.

Exploring these intertwined worlds in the immediacy of school brings about realizations like the one shared by one of my former students who exclaimed, "I didn't know this existed in our community". Finding new meaning through community dialogue contains the hope of teaching as an organizer: that through discovering the social ties that bind us together we learn to value one another. In valuing one another, we learn to respect the richness of living together, learning together and acting together. As we expand our knowledge of others and self, of individuality and collectivity, we think about our surroundings and wonder aloud with our friends, new and old, we summon the creativity and togetherness needed to address issues of great importance to all our lives.

Where Does a Guest Speaker Fit Within the Progression of Learning in a Unit?

Guest partners can boost the salience of learning in a unit. Previously, we've discussed the sequence of learning activities within a unit through the use of the "mountain model" as a planning tool. Thinking about the primary issue(s) within a unit and starting with how those issues are affecting local life is a great place to start. From this starting point, consider how students might begin to access and interact with various kinds of data, including experiential data gathering and activities, which help students to construct their own knowledge. This phase of inquiry fits with the concepts of "agitation" and "education" from the AEIOU framework. Guest partners can bring up new ideas, which help us dig deeper and further our education on the issue. Yet, it is common to use the guests only once initial knowledge has been established among the learners. For that reason, I have come to see guest speakers, in many ways, as facilitators of the "inoculation" phase of the AEIOU organizing framework.

Guest speakers fit within the "inoculation" phase of the organizing framework largely because of what they represent. The guest speaker represents a "small dose" of the real world. They are not representative of the entire adult world outside of school, but rather are a perspective—a portal between the learner and the adults. As a small dose of the adult world, the guest brings an "outsider" view of the issues. They bring more nuisance and extended experience with the issue. Understanding this allows us to leverage the guest's time toward the overarching goals of the unit.

Guest speakers can be a test point for student knowledge. Student knowledge has been gathered and constructed within the school setting up to the point at which the guest joins the class. This means that the guest is the first chance for the students to test their knowledge, to verify that what they have found stands up against the experience of experts and the larger communal understanding of an issue.

The public introduction of the guest to the class through the formal reading of the presenter's biography by the learners is a "credentialing" of the expert. It establishes the guest's experience beyond the uncritical explanation, "They are here because my teacher invited them". The presentation of the guest's credentials then invites the learners to appraise the relevance of the guest's experience in light of their own knowledge of the topic—and in so doing enter into a larger community of learners.

Students can then try to puzzle over and fit whatever the guest shared into their understanding of an issue. Since the guest is a guest, we often invite them to speak first, to share about their work. One guest, a mother of a student, spoke with a class about being a woman in a male-dominant profession, the building trades. Her son later reflected that he had never heard about the challenges that his mother faced before. Entering into a community of learners by sharing her story in a public setting provided the son with a chance to puzzle over the mother he knew in the private setting of the family and the strong professional woman who he now saw in the public setting. A lifetime of experience in the private setting did not reveal what a morning in the public setting made clear, as the students said, his mom was a "boss". The puzzling together of knowledge through interacting with guests from the community begs students to ask questions about the generalizability of their knowledge, "If this is true, how much further does this idea extend?" and "If this is true, what else do I need to rethink?"

Students can then move from adding the new things that they hear into their existing pool of knowledge to sharing what they have discovered on their own. Students can assess the strength of their discoveries even when sharing the smallest increment of their knowledge with a guest. Of course, the more that students share, the more feedback the guests can provide. The exchange of ideas is the foundation of the wider community of learners. Sampling the feedback that they receive from guests points the students toward what they need to do next in their study, how they can iterate ideas and how they can prepare for increasing their capacity to share more: whether going from sharing nothing to a tidbit, from a tidbit to an example or from an example to a fully developed idea.

The very presence of the guest in school tells the students that what they are learning holds importance outside of the classroom. This is encouraging for learners. The presence of the guest also tells students that it is safe to bring an idea forward. If it is safe to share with a guest, then it's okay to bring the inquiry further—to make it more real. In this regard, the guest is a gateway to more organizing and to the "getting organized" phase of the AEIOU framework. Integrating the feedback and lessons learned from the guest moves students toward refining their ideas and toward being ready to take the next steps up the "mountain" of learning. As teachers, our integration of guests into the classroom allows for us to feel how positioning experts and community voices into the unit can bring learning to this next level.

The Observational Site Visit

Waste Treatment Plant (Observational Site Visit)

Dondero School Elementary School is located in Portsmouth, New Hampshire. The school is named for the first female mayor of Portsmouth and New Hampshire, Mary C. Dondero, whose photo hangs in the school's lobby. At Dondero Elementary, the core of a team of fifth grade teachers, Jen O'Mahony and Molly French, worked together for nearly 20 years. Over the course of that time, they have developed a curriculum they call "Summit to Sea" where they integrate science, social studies, reading and writing. Their work exemplifies how place-based learning and observational site visits can be a powerful tool for learning, using the everyday places of our lives as catalysts of curiosity and engagement.

Pierce Island is defined by water. Water surrounds it on nearly all sides with an access road connecting it to the mainland, close to the historic colonial settlement of Strawbery Banke. For most fifth graders in the City of Portsmouth, the island is known for being the home to the public Pierce

Island pool—an escape from the summer heat. As many of those fifth grade visitors to the pool discover, the island is also home to the City's Wastewater Treatment Plant, which they often refer to as "the poop factory".

Smell is often one of the first things students recall when they find out that the class is going to visit Piece Island as part of their "Summit to Sea" learning.

It was a foggy day during the 2025 visit to the Plant—the air felt thick and heavy. As the school bus made its way over the bridge from the mainland and up the island, students peered out the "cloudy" windows of the yellow school bus to point out the pool. They claimed to smell something funny.

"Pierce Island Signage" outside the wastewater treatment facility.

As students filed off the bus, many took a big inhale. Students were half disappointed and half relieved to find that there wasn't much of a smell at all—other than the waft of sea breeze that struggled to move much of the dense fog that still surrounded the island. Several students had brought masks with them, expecting the smell to be overbearing. Most of these they quietly pocketed, while a few students still felt the need for an extra layer of protection, a feeling that everyone could understand.

Waiting at the entrance, the classes met up with their tour guide, an engineer named Keith. "Where's the smell?" the students immediately asked Keith. He greeted the classes and then informed them that he had flushed the pipes yesterday, which was likely why the aroma in the area was less pungent. The students were intrigued.

Keith signaled for everyone to follow him. Four classes of ten-year-olds marched right into the Wastewater Treatment Center. The first stop: the control room. One student described it as "a lot of buttons". Keith reminded the students not to touch the buttons and that the buttons and gauges helped him to monitor the treatment of the water.

The reminder of the importance of the glowing buttons drew out several observations and questions from the students. The most notable of these was that several boys had noticed on the way inside that the water treatment plant was surrounded by a tall fence that had barbed wire on top of it. Keith confirmed that the fence did have barbed wire and that it was meant to keep the facility safe. "The water treatment center is an important part of our community infrastructure–it helps to keep people, animals and the environment safe and healthy", he said. The boys nodded knowingly.

Moving down the corridor, Keith, the engineer, explained that when we flushed the toilet at school or ran the faucet at home, the water and everything it carried traveled down into pipes that were buried underground. Those pipes ran all over the city and came together into larger pipes that eventually traveled to the Water Treatment Plant. Standing on top of a grate, Keith pointed to large pipes that lay under his feet. Some of the pipes were as wide as five feet in diameter—exceeding the height of many in the class. Keith flipped up a grate and revealed a portal through which students could see the water and waste coming into the facility from the city. The class saw the water rushing through along with bits of solids.

Inside the Peirce Island Wastewater Treatment Center.

Walking further, Keith described how the untreated water, once in the plant, would make its first stop. This "phase one" of the filtration system removed paper and large objects from the water. Students saw rods swirling around the water with belts pulling out solids.

Next, with the large solids gone, the water went to the "g-stage". Again, a small viewing window allowed brave students to view the process. Those who stood on tiptoes said they saw what looked to be a "bunch of corn". These smaller corn-like solids were then extracted from the water.

"Observing Grit" student is lifted up to look inside the tube of wastewater.

"Ready for the sludge pool?" Keith asked. It was a moment of trepidation for some—a moment of pure curiosity for many. Those two words, "Sludge pool", summoned all kinds of images. Students opened the nearby door and walked outside. The reality was large containers with open tops filled with the water. A mechanical arm circled the top of the containers, skimming the sludge off on the top. The students were disturbed to see seagulls enjoying diving into the sludge pools. The seagulls acted at home: splashing around, dabbling and acting as though they hadn't a care in the world.

Suits hung on a wall nearby. They looked like wetsuits with various devices of dive gear attached—pressure gauges, breathing masks, etc. Many students wanted to know what would happen if you fell into the sludge pool. But, the suits were not for rescue operations and did not belong to the on-call extraction team for wayward visitors. The suits were there for cleaning out the "vessels", which had just recently been done.

Unsure if it was a good thing that there was no on-call rescue team—the classes proceeded to the biggest building of all at the plant. It was the building that held the "compactor". The compactor took the sludge that had been skimmed off at the sludge pool and compacted it into big bricks. The bricks were the size of cars. Trucks came and took the bricks away from the facility. There, the students saw the compressors and the compacting of the sludge into bricks.

The second room in the big building had hundreds of vats. Students noticed that a company called "Tyler" produced these industrial vats. In the "Tyler" vats, water was being treated with chemicals prior to its release.

Taking a break from all the action, everyone traveled to the rooftop of the facility to take in the view—it was possible to see the harbor, the river and the city. Keith shared that it's where he and his coworkers sometimes liked to eat lunch.

Finally, students traveled down to the release point for the treated water. The water traveled through a maze of pipes, was treated with chlorine and then headed over a waterfall into the Piscataqua River below.

Before leaving, the classes made one last stop to talk with the scientists at the plant. Keith told the class that the Wastewater Plant has a higher level of code enforcement because it was an environmentally sensitive area. The plant had been built in the 1960s and had been upgraded many times over the years, including most recently in 2021. These upgrades and the work of the scientists to maintain a high level of integrity meet federal regulations like the Clean Water Act, the students were assured. Beakers, droppers and testing instruments around the room caught the eyes of students.

Students noticed there was a fridge in the room and asked if that was where the employees kept their lunches. No, the scientists replied, the fridge was for holding scientific samples from the treatment plant. And with that, the student departed for the bus and then had lunch back at school.

In the days that followed, students reflected on their visit to the Peirce Island Wastewater Treatment Plant. Taking what they learned at the Plant, the students designed their own filtration systems. Teachers provided students with silty water and the students tried different techniques for straining and extracting sediments. Teams tested their designs, made adjustments and reconfigured their models to try and create the most effective filter system.

The team of teachers took photos throughout their study, including photos of the site visit to the Wastewater Treatment Plant and photos of the filter designing and testing process. They shared these photos with students' families in their newsletter—lifting up the great work of the students and giving each student's adult a chance to have a conversation with their students about their learning.

Students work to create their own filtration systems.

Preparing for Observational Site Visits

Identifying a strand in the curriculum can be the place to start when preparing for a site visit. The fifth grade teachers at Dondero identified the study of water as a resource as a throughline for teaching science. From there, they considered the local places that demonstrably were tied to the use and stewardship of water. Their visit to the Wastewater Treatment Plant had been preceded by studies of water and water systems that dated back to the start of the year and their kick-off climb up Mount Agamenticus, in nearby York, Maine. At the top of "Mount A", as the students call it, you have the rare view of both Maine and New Hampshire's Atlantic coastline, but on a clear day, you can also see northward all the way to the White Mountains. The hike and the view are a panoramic preview of the lessons for the year as the students go with the flow of the water, eventually all the way out to Pierce Island and the Piscataqua River.

Before the Wastewater Treatment Plant visit could take place, it helped that the teachers had a "big view" of their curriculum. Starting with a vision of a curriculum that centered hands-on experiences for learners engaging with the community, they slowly added experiences over the years. Developing a contact within the Wastewater Treatment Facility, getting approval for the visit from the site managers and the school administration, as well as doing the work of completing the necessary permission forms and scheduling transportation was all part of logistical arrangements for the visit. Once the team of teachers had run the trip once, the logistical elements of the trip were documented and filed, allowing the team to take the trip in the next year without recreating everything.

Our knowledge of our grade level helps us in planning site visits. Students in late childhood and early adolescents are in the phase of development where they are increasingly interested in the world and how it works. There is a playfulness in how they voice their displeasure with smells and sights that are pungent, rotting or generally unappealing. This playfulness opens an avenue of interest for engaging with community issues that are both highly relevant to our lives and "very gross". The teacher's knowledge of this unique combination set the stage for engaged learning and the use of site visits as memorable teaching tools that can be referred to long after the visit.

While the casual observer might make the mistake of seeing the visit to the Wastewater Treatment Plant as "just a field trip", the truth is that it is an artful display of the teacher's skill at developing a community partnership that fits both the curriculum and student interests. The teachers intentionally developed the observational site visit to the Wastewater Treatment Facility after living and working in the community for years. Their involvement and long-term engagement with the community allowed them to try different visits and learn from various partners. This learning honed their "teachers' gut" and their sense of what was actually "do-able" rather than getting stuck in thinking about "what was possible". In this regard, it's important to consider the trajectory of your curriculum, your year and your career and not to overextend yourself in creating partnerships for site visits that might limit your future capacity. Pick one experience, try it out and build on it.

When Do Observational Site Visits Fit into the Sequence of a Unit?

Observational site visits give students real-world models for their work. Students can see processes that otherwise might feel abstract in action during site visits. The observational site visit when tied to the local area shows students how things work in their own community. While site visits, like guest partners, can be agitational, they typically fit well in the "education" phase and the "getting organized" phase of AEIOU framework.

Site visits are educational in the sense that they demonstrate how things work in the real world. It's not theoretical knowledge, it's where the rubber meets the road. Along these lines, from an organizer's perspective, the site visit has an element of teaching students about power dynamics. In this regard, the following questions are present: Who is in control? How do people work together? What are the costs and benefits of the systems at play at the site? These are questions that don't all have clear answers when you haven't seen the workings of a place firsthand. The site visit puts students in conversation with people who have real needs and who are working within systems today. These are all educational elements of the site visit that otherwise might be skimmed over and go unnoticed.

Site visits also help students to visualize what it looks like to "get organized" in a particular line of work. In other words, it gives students a living model of: who does what, where and when? Encountering the living model in person and getting to interact with it is an initial testing ground for students. Activating student's prior knowledge of a site-based model before traveling for an observation allows students to more readily compare their pre-visit conceptualization of the model to the actual workings of the site. Students test their background knowledge by collecting data (both formal and informal) while on site. This can look like asking questions, gathering data on a worksheet and/or using their senses to be attune to the full site experience. In this respect, even what may appear to be the simplest observation or question should be honored as an attempt to integrate new data into the student's existing knowledge.

The durability of the integrated knowledge should be further tested upon returning back to the classroom. Students can use the experience to demonstrate their more nuanced understanding of how things work, how people work together and relevant content application to ongoing studies. Students can synthesize their knowledge when presented with a post-observation related task. This is a synthesis of their prior knowledge, the observations made at the site, the comparisons between their prior knowledge and their observations all within the context of a related task.

Place-based site observations increase relevance of student learning. The Wastewater Treatment visit of the fifth graders of the Dondero School exemplifies how a place-based site visit can have a lingering effect on daily behavior. Not only did the students learn about the coordinated effort to treat and release wastewater, but they also learned how they are each individually linked to a complex system and a critical public service. Even as a young person, they are forever reminded of their site visit each time they turn on a tap, flush the toilet or go for a swim. That daily reminder brings students back to their responsibility to be stewards of the water and other natural resources—both out of their own self-interest and for future generations.

Site-based visits are a powerful tool for teaching like an organizer. They are the meeting point of the "world as it is" and "world as it should be" for students. So much about our modern world is taken for granted, especially the conveniences we use each day, like running water. For many, running water is like magic—something that we just enjoy and don't really need to try to explain. This kind of magical thinking is the kind of naivete that impedes progress. Site visits, like the Wastewater Treatment Plant, show us the hard work that goes into supporting our lives and inspire us to take on the challenges of advancing technologies like filtration systems that can help both our community and communities around the world. This is how teaching like an organizer can leverage the everyday places closeby to grow both mindsets and skill sets that bring about positive change.

The Beekeeper (Reciprocal)

Public schools play an essential role in restoring common ground in our communities. This is because public schools are for everyone. They are places of learning built on principles of "liberty and justice for all"—words recited every morning in schools across the United States. These principles are lived out in our schools and in the pursuit of creating communities surrounding our schools that address issues that help create a stronger, more vibrant community, which in turn creates stronger and more vibrant schools. This virtuous cycle is one that starts in classrooms like that of fourth grade teacher, Mrs. Sarah McCain.

Her class was curious to know about the humble bee. SeaBee Honey (2021), a local business based on the Seacoast of New Hampshire that is "dedicated to the preservation of the honey bee and all native pollinators in the New England area…", was a match for Mrs. McCain's class. Seabees, which provides all kinds of material and educational support to schools in the area that are interested in bee life, worked with the class to write a grant that helped bring bees to the school.

A local Seabee beekeeper worked with Ms. McCain's class to create and learn more about hive life through firsthand experiences. The students wanted to know: What would it look like to keep bees in a schoolyard? Would children be afraid of bees? Would it limit outdoor time? Together, the class and the beekeeper discussed the details. A little courtyard-like alcove was selected as the best site for a class hive.

Students learned from the beekeeper about the process of keeping bees. Some dawned the beekeeper suit in the classroom and others ventured out to the alcove to assist with live bees. Students learned about the "smoker" and "frames" and how to extract honey from the frames. The honey that the class harvested from the frames was jarred, labeled and sold to parents and the community. SeaBee Honey benefitted from the project by creating relationships and placing hives that directly supported their mission. By hosting hives and by growing out native pollinator gardens, the school was helping local farms and farmers throughout the region.

The class later worked with the non-profit "The Bee Cause" as a fundraiser for materials to support beekeeping at the school. Through the partnership with "The Bee Cause", in coordination with the school's Parent Teacher Organization, students sold bottles of 100% wildflower honey to parents and community members for $15, with $5 going to local school programs and $10 going to help support other schools and community-based organizations with similar programing (2023).

Successive classes participated in this partnership and other grades joined in by growing bee gardens. Teachers linked the experiences with the bees to the science curriculum at the school—and the work supported reading and writing as well. Students joined the morning announcements from the beekeeping class to share facts about the bees.

Sadly, one of the facts the class found out about (and later shared) was the devastating effect of bee mites. Bee mites feed off their host, the bee, and can lead to the complete collapse of a hive. After several years of the colony needing to be replaced, a costly endeavor, the difficult decision was made to pause the collaborative program. Still, this provided a window into the potential of a reciprocal model for community partnership that enhanced student learning through a sweet community partnership.

Reflection Questions:
- How did the class use the AEIOU framework?
- Are there grants that can support your partnerships?
- What do you see as the trade-offs from the teacher perspective in terms of investing time and resources into a reciprocal partnership vs. a guest or a site visit?
- How does an on-site partnership enhance mentorship?

Photo: Bee Board from Ms. McCain's class.

Preparing for Observational Reciprocal Partnerships

When it comes to reciprocal partnerships, in addition to the scouting out of local associations at gatherings, it can help to conduct a search online of associations and non-profits that have a mission related to your learning. Create a list of the contact information for potential partners and then work through the list by reaching out to contacts to see if there might be congruence.

A relationship that might start with a partner coming in as a guest speaker can evolve to be more of a long-term commitment when there is the right fit. It can work out that local associations know about grants or other resources that can help grow and sustain a partnership like Seabees. Local associations may also have staff members or volunteers who can help write or even be the primary authors of grants.

Our openness and commitment to exploring partnerships of this kind can bring about opportunities that otherwise might be unforeseen at the start of our planning work. This can take a considerable time investment upfront in making contact and developing relationships in a manner that explores what your class can do with the partner. Yet, the mission-focused work of non-profits is a perfect zone for organizing as each non-profit has an explicitly stated vision for the "world as it should be". This is an invitation to the teacher, as an organizer on the ground, to show the non-profit how the school exists in the "world as it is" and ask for the non-profit to partner in an effort to bring us closer to their stated vision. Such a conversation must be conducted in the spirit of shared values and collaboration—always seeking to strengthen both the position of the non-profit and the learning mission of the school.

When Do Reciprocal Partnerships Fit into the Sequence of a Unit?

Reciprocal partnerships can fit different needs for teaching like an organizer. The physical location of the partnership can determine the frequency of direct learning experiences.

Proximity increases the ability to return to the site of learning. When a partnership is based on school grounds or has activities that can be based on school grounds, there can be increased recursivity within the unit. For example, we might start off taking inventory of the native plants and flowers on our school grounds (agitation), move to talking about the lack of biodiversity with our partner (education), before continuing to track whether seasonality affects the variety of native blooms (organizing/coordination). This can lead to an ongoing educational conversation with the partner and more of an in-depth study, which is agitational and gets us thinking about what other actions we need to take. This back and forth of dialogue and discovery leads to action that is catalyzed by the proximity and availability of partners. School-site learning paired with partner flexibility increases responsiveness for learners. Continuing the example, the partner can then consult with students about types of flowers that they would like to introduce to the schoolyard based on their research. In this role, the partner, like the guest speaker, is playing the part of helping the students to figure out what will really work and what might be too challenging—a form of inoculation from the AEIOU framework.

Since the site of learning is the school, students are able to puzzle and mess about with "getting organized". In the planting of native flowers, this might mean identifying the best places for the flowers based on exposure to the sun throughout the day, mapping out existing gardens, tracking known wildlife patterns at the school and coordinating with the custodial staff. "Getting organized" on the school grounds also means figuring out where to get the seeds or starter packs for flowers, who will plant them, when they'll be planted and who will water them. All of these logistical questions can more easily play out at school when the school ground is the site of the learning because of the ease of access that proximity permits.

On the other hand, limitations can be overcome for reciprocal partnerships, including partner availability and distance. Partners with less schedule flexibility can use a mix of digital and in-person appearances to continue to assist the class. This kind of arrangement can also be helpful for partners who are coming from further away.

Distance between the partner and the school may limit the opportunity for the students to "give back" at the site of the partner through acts of volunteerism and service. This kind of challenge can be overcome by scheduling the site visit at the end of the unit, as a form of "uplifting" the work of the students and in celebration of the partnership. The service becomes a way for students learning to directly impact the community and help the partner organization.

Ultimately, time and availability for both the class and the partner will determine what we can accomplish together in a given year. With this in mind, accounting for the sequencing of lessons and partner engagements provides avenues for approaching reciprocal partnerships. What may appear to be a limitation at first may in fact give us another perspective on how a partner best fits into our plans—while also hopefully fitting theirs.

When teaching like an organizer, we look for partners in the community who align with our curriculum, who can enhance student learning and who may benefit from engaging with our students. Searching out and developing partnerships that are based in reciprocity is one of the surest paths to forging long-term, healthy and sustainable partnerships. Such partnerships build strength between schools as public institutions of learning and other civic institutions and associations.

Strong partnerships, in turn, create the dynamic that cultivates a healthier civic ecosystem for our communities. Years ago, during a summer program, I was working with high school students on a service learning project in the Pilsen neighborhood of Chicago. There, we collaborated with a team of volunteers who helped run a community garden. The garden was located between what had once been heavy industry and rail lines—a history that was reflected on the "Gears to gardens" mural (see above). Due to its industrial past, the community had opted to grow their veggies and flowers in raised beds, keeping their roots away from possible contamination in the soil. After a day of mulching, the garden volunteers invited us to see their beehives, which they had added to their garden through a grant (shown below).

Beehives at a community garden in Pilsen, Chicago.

The hive helped pollinate the garden, which brought healthy food to the community. The garden also served as an afterschool program for young people. I share this story because I think it speaks to the good work that is being done in communities all over the country.

Everyday folks are considering how to take on issues like access to healthy food, clean water and environmental protection. The fact is this work isn't being done from the top-down, but rather from the grassroots being led by teachers and public servants, volunteers and concerned citizens. The pattern of working to improve community outcomes for these issues are similar too—it follows the organizing model laid out in this book.

Now, what if we shared these stories to inspire and to provide reassurance that we are not the only ones doing this? What if we took the practices that we are already engaged with and kept taking the next step and then another? Our common pursuits and methods, as well as our commitment to taking that next step, especially in times of heightened fear when it feels like anything outside of conformity may land us in trouble, is what keeps each one of us going. And if we suffer setbacks, if our beehives are overtaken by mites or revenue streams dry up, we can take heart that there are people teaching like organizers all over this country and world. That fact can help us reconnect to the good work that is being humbly advanced by people like all of us in every community.

Expanding Teaching Like an Organizer Within Our Schools

Practicing teaching like an organizer is the practice of democracy. It's the work of creating community through relational living. "Democracy must begin at home", Dewey wrote, "and its home is the neighborly community" (2012). For this reason, expanding the practice of teaching like an organizer requires that we look to act and expand our actions locally. In the context of being a teacher who spends a significant amount of his working hours in school, this means acting within school to nurture the kind of organizing practices that strengthen democratic culture, expanding the ideas discussed in this book.

Professional development or "in service" days are one of the traditional ways that schools have tried to assist teachers in acquiring new skills and to give us time to hone our practice. The trouble is that professional development is often hours of sitting with very little usable information imparted. As teachers, we often feel more depleted at the end of a day of "PD" (professional development) than at the end of our typical day with students. In short, professional development has traditionally not been a model for what teaching can look like. Which is why we should ask: What if we approached professional development as teachers who organize?

We feel so drained after professional development because it doesn't fit our daily needs—professional development is often this island that you arrive on as if shipwrecked. Washed ashore, you look around and instead of life preservers you find the remnants of poppy seed bagels, if you're lucky. You grip your coffee cup with an intensity of one who clings to the last canteen of potable water.

Now, what if professional development was a feature of community learning rather than a barren island? Perhaps this could be a remedy—so let's first consider what makes this island so untenable.

Too much professional development is lecture based. We're teachers. We can't help but feel the immense contradiction in our bones: we are being lectured to by folks brought in by our bosses. Lectures can be fine in and of themselves under the right circumstances. During professional development, rarely is the right circumstance. Why? Because when an outside expert is brought into any community, it is extremely difficult for that expert to inform the members of the community on how to improve at doing their job without implicitly telling the people within the community that they don't know how to do their job. As a form of communication that is predominantly one-directional (from speaker to audience), the lecture places authority in the speaker—diminishing the authority of the audience. This is why many effective guest speakers seek ways to either have the audience grant consent for a lecture or seek to structure their engagement through more dialogue-based forms of communication.

Professional development is often put together by non-teachers. If you are outside of the classroom, it's hard to know what the people on the inside want and need. Most of us just want some extra time to grade the last assignment and prepare for upcoming lessons. That said, professional development planned by non-teachers is often reliant on outside experts who have not been in the classroom for some time, or who have not lived the particulars of our daily lives as teachers. This is maybe more true in the post-COVID world than ever as the speed of change in schools has increased so rapidly in this time. In total, this means that professional development is often built on assumptions about the needs of the classroom teacher rather than the real needs of the classroom teacher.

The dissonance between assumed needs and real needs perpetuates a paternalism in the school system, often despite good intentions on the part of the planners of professional development. It disincentives teachers from owning their learning with the assertion that someone else knows what you need better than you know what you need. If you think about being subjected to this message for years over the course of your career, there is little wonder why professional development can be such a tricky topic in education. We have been trained with the message: check your experience and needs at the door.

What Would It Mean to Flip the Script on Professional Development?

Flipping the script on professional development is a way to amplify the concepts of teaching like an organizer. Why? Teaching like an organizer is all about the needs, the issues and the experiences of the people with whom we are in community. Professional development should affirm the lives that we live and the experiences we have. The simple starting place would be in the communities we serve.

At a minimum, this means surveying the staff about what they want to learn about and what they need time to do. These actions can all be tied to the visions and strategic goals of the school or district. Teachers can self-group based on survey results and move to the learning group that speaks to their needs.

Over time, these interest groups could also form into long-term learning communities of their own where teachers can study aspects of practice and content knowledge that are meaningful to the practitioners. These long-term learning groups would help us to move away from professional development that is a "one and done" session. Rather, guests could be invited by the long-term learning groups when a new voice or a different perspective is needed, allowing for the teachers as learners to keep a sense of continuity in their own learning community.

Teaching like an organizer is rooted in what is possible today, which means that we have to be real about the patchwork landscape that is professional development. In schools where long-term learning groups are not yet possible, teachers can request to lead their own community-based professional development within a block of time on the day scheduled for in-service training. I've made this proposal and called it "Exploring Town". The proposal asks the district to provide teachers with two to three hours to explore the downtown of the local community. In the process, teachers aim to have one-on-one conversations with community members through venturing into shops and walking in public places. We walk and talk with local people, gain new contacts in the community and identify sites of interest and issues in the broader community.

Finding connections to the communities that support our schools is a way to refine our practice alongside our fellow educators. It breathes fresh air into professional development. We're asserting that training comes not from expert "outsiders" but from teachers working outside side by side with colleagues to make learning, as Dewey (1916) said "life itself".

Walking the neighborhoods and downtown creates a mental map in our minds of the area. Travel the routes that colleagues walked as they grew up. Travel the sidewalks our students take to and from school. Travel by foot to allow yourself to serendipitously bump into an old acquaintance, or to meet the "stranger" who is just a friend waiting to be made. Physical activity places us directly on the path of public learning.

You can use the following statements and questions to help organize your community walk:

- ♦ I'm a teacher at _____ school and we're trying to make connections to the community for students. Could you tell me about your store/organization?

- Did you or anyone you know go to the school? What was it like then?
- We're interested in improving our connections to the community. Would you be interested in collaborating on a project with students? We will be learning about…

Also, stay organized as you go:

- Keep a record of new contacts.
- Keep a record of points of interest in the community.
- Send thank you notes to anyone who might have expressed interest in working with the school and students.
- Share your list and ideas with colleagues to increase your points of contact and to assess the viability of ideas.

Just like professional development cannot be an island, school shouldn't be either. Getting out and being in the community sends a new message about learning for both adults and students. When given the opportunity to bring our full selves to the work of learning, we open the door to amazing new connections and opportunities.

We are doing the work with each step.

Works Cited

The Bee Cause Project – Charleston, SC. (2023). The Bee Cause Project. https://www.thebeecause.org/

Dewey, J. (2012). *The public and its problems: An essay in political inquiry.* In Melvin L. Rogers (Ed.) (p. 157). Penn State University Press.

Dewey, J. (1916). *Democracy and education: An introduction to the philosophy of education.* Free Pr.

Ganz, M. (2020). *Why stories matter: The art and craft of social change.* Retrieved July 30, 2021, from https://commonslibrary.org/why-stories-matter-the-art-and-craft-of-social-change/#:~:text=Marshall Ganz, key community organising, Self, Us and Now).

Goodwin, J. (2024). *Conversation and conservation: Using open-ended inquiry to co-create learning | Social studies. Middle level learning, 79.* National Council for the Social Studies. https://www.socialstudies.org/79/conversation-and-conservation-using-open-ended-inquiry-co-create-learning

Peirce Island Wastewater Facility. (2017). *City of Portsmouth.* https://www.portsmouthnh.gov/publicworks/wastewater/peirce-island-wastewater-facility

SeaBee Honey. (2021). SEABEE HONEY; Twelve Shares Natural Foods LLC. https://seabeehoney.com/index.html

For Product Safety Concerns and Information please contact our EU
representative GPSR@taylorandfrancis.com
Taylor & Francis Verlag GmbH, Kaufingerstraße 24, 80331 München, Germany

www.ingramcontent.com/pod-product-compliance
Lightning Source LLC
Chambersburg PA
CBHW052019070526
44584CB00016B/1822